AF378569

Ritual and Custom
of Ancient Cultures

Professor Deng Qiyao
Photography: Cat Vinton
Translation: Wu Fan and Will Spence
Executive Editor: Xue Xinran

China

Adorned

Page 1: A Kham Tibetan woman with coral and turquoise accessories attending Losar new year celebrations in Dege County, Garze Tibetan Autonomous Prefecture, Sichuan.

Contents

Note on Translation

This book celebrates the diversity of China, not least its many languages. Although it has been translated directly from the Chinese, many of the original sources and accounts on which the book is based are themselves translations of regional languages and dialects. In several instances, the names of religious festivals, musical instruments, items of clothing and mythological figures were first phoneticised into Chinese. Chinese terms that appear in the text have been transliterated according to the standard Pinyin system of Romanisation. And in some cases, additional information has been included to help explain and contextualise cultural concepts that may be unfamiliar to Western readers.

The concept of *minzu* is central to this book, but it is a difficult one to translate. Whereas 'nationality' was used in the past, *minzu* is now commonly rendered as 'ethnic group'. There is even a growing tendency to leave the word untranslated and adopt it into our own vocabulary. This ambiguity not only reflects the trials of translation, but also the evolving relationship between China and the fifty-five non-Han ethnic groups, who make up around 8 per cent of the country's population. For the sake of clarity, we have used 'ethnic group' when referring to the fifty-six ethnic groups recognised by the People's Republic of China, and 'ethnic minority' when referring to the fifty-five non-Han ethnic groups, such as the Yi, Miao and Hani.

While a translation can never be completely faithful to the original, we hope to have captured at least something of Professor Deng's eloquence in his native language, and the passion with which he approaches his subject.

Note on Ethnic Groups

The names of the fifty-six officially recognised ethnic groups – and their numerous subgroups – vary widely. Some of the minority groups in this book may self-identify under different names; for clarity, we chose to keep naming conventions consistent throughout the text. Wherever possible, we translated the names that inform our understanding of the group's heritage (such as Longhorn Miao, Flowery Yi or Black-Sand Zhuang). For names without a clear English translation (such as Hani Aini or Kavalan Gaoshan), we opted for transliteration.

Note on Photography

The black-and-white images in *China Adorned* are drawn from Professor Deng Qiyao's archive, which spans three decades of research on the cultural traditions of China's ethnic groups. These photographs (all taken by Deng unless otherwise credited) offer a rare view into often-remote communities, recording ways of life that are changing rapidly and, in some cases, no longer exist. His archival imagery is interspersed with contemporary shots by ethnographic photographer Cat Vinton, who captured the rituals, surrounding landscapes and daily life of ethnic minority groups in Yunnan, Qinghai, Sichuan and Guizhou provinces in 2018.

Previous: The Duoyishu rice terraces at sunrise in Yuanyang County, Honghe Hani and Yi Autonomous Prefecture, Yunnan. For more than 1300 years, the Hani people have sculpted the terraces (or *titian*), drawing water from the forested mountains for use in agriculture.

Introduction

The first time my mind turned to the question of clothing was in the 1960s. During that time anything 'old' or 'foreign' was bad, certain types of clothing included. My mother's high-heeled shoes soon disappeared from her wardrobe, and, out on the streets in my home province of Yunnan, some people were ready to confront anyone wearing trousers they deemed too tight. Carrying rice-wine bottles, they would seize unsuspecting passers-by and try to stuff a bottle inside their trouser leg. Torn trousers would be considered getting off lightly. Those not so lucky were arrested, detained, denounced, beaten and publicly humiliated.

I was in my early teens at the start of the Cultural Revolution. At the time, fashion meant a choice between an army uniform or a so-called Mao suit. Public meetings were always drab affairs; people would mockingly refer to themselves as the 'grey and blue ants'. Young as I was back then, I simply thought this was the colour of the world.

In the late 1960s and 70s, China's schools were shuttered, and millions of young people were sent from their urban homes to the countryside. For us *zhiqing*, 'sent-down youth', it was both our great misfortune and fortune to be directed to the outer regions of the country – areas largely populated by ethnic minorities – to be 'reformed' through rural labour. We may have missed out on formal education, but we discovered another world.

I was sent to the China–Myanmar border, home to many different ethnic groups. The clothes they wore were a stark contrast to the boxy, dull attire I was used to back home among my Han peers (China's majority ethnicity, representing more than 90 per cent of the population). Women of the Dai, Jingpo, Achang and De'ang minorities wore short tops and sarong-style *tongqun* dresses. Though distinctive in terms of material, pattern and colour, their clothes were all close-fitting and intricately decorated.

The women of the Aini, a branch of the Hani ethnic group, wore dresses that revealed their midriff and legs, and on their heads they displayed a medley of ornaments made of feathers, bone, flowers and insects. I couldn't believe what I was seeing. These women opened my eyes to the colour of the world and showed me that the desire to decorate ourselves in the name of beauty is part of human nature.

The next time clothing moved me in this way was when I began my anthropological research. I had gone back to university in 1978 and studied Chinese language and literature. But the minority cultures I had encountered during my time in the countryside were never far from my mind. There was still so much I wanted to understand, and I finally found my calling in ethnographic research in the mid-1980s.

On one field trip to a Miao village in central Yunnan, I visited the village elders, seeking insights into their community. An old man asked me:

'Can you read?'

I was dumbstruck. *Why is he asking that?* I thought.

The old man pointed at a young girl wearing traditional dress. 'Our ancestral heritage is written here', he said.

There were no words written on the clothes, just a sequence of beautiful designs, both embroidered and printed in wax. Only then did I realise that I couldn't 'read' a word.

Seeing my confusion, the old man proceeded to explain all the different decorative motifs. He pointed out which imagery spoke of the creation myth, which patterns were in fact records of their ancestors' migration from the Yellow River region of China, which stitching had come from whose needle, and which colours were bound to a person's faith (and fate).

China covers a vast territory, roughly equivalent to the whole of Europe. The topography and climates are diverse, the vegetation rich and varied. As I travelled further afield, discovering the sparkling brilliance of many ethnic groups'

traditional dress, I grew to admire the harmony between clothing, culture and environment. Minorities from the great plateaus and deserts wear thick coats of heavy-set fur and felt; minorities from the coast and the river valleys wear flowing, elegant and supple textiles; and those along the Silk Road wear garments as colourful as the rainbow. As for minorities in the Tibetan–Yi Corridor, their clothing is so richly ornamented that it's like visiting a moveable museum.

The distribution of ethnic groups across China is complex, the boundaries by no means clear-cut. For example, the Yellow and Yangtze river basins in the east, known as a Han region, are also home to many ethnic minority communities. Conversely, in the west and north where most minorities live, there are plenty of Han settlements. Much of my research has been concentrated in Yunnan, China's most ethnically diverse province. Of the country's fifty-six officially recognised ethnic groups, fifty-two have a presence in Yunnan. The folk cultures there can trace their roots back to ancient human civilisation.

Each Chinese ethnic group has its own unique traditional dress. When Westerners think of traditional Chinese clothing, what usually comes to mind is either the wide-sleeved, flowing robes of the Han tradition or the form-fitting *qipao* (*cheongsam*) dress that originated during Manchu rule. This is the attire that dominates in the media and popular culture, so it's unsurprising that even many Han Chinese know little about the diverse costumes and customs of other ethnic groups.

China's ethnic minorities are by no means homogenous either. Even within a single minority, there might be a number of different branches. Each branch – each village, even – has a clothing system in its own right. It is common for an ethnic group to have hundreds of different types of traditional clothing, all meticulously handmade using a multitude of materials and in a variety of shapes. The craftsmanship evident in their work often confounds professional artists and designers, and the way in which these clothes and adornments embody the culture is equally astounding.

Nearly all ethnic groups use clothing as a kind of wordless communication. The Jingpo minority have a saying: 'Everything under heaven is woven onto our dress, the words left by our ancestors.' Much of history is recorded with the written word. But in ancient times, when there was no written word, and among certain ethnic minorities with no written language, history was and continues to be 'written' in a number of ways. The needle is the pen and the thread the ink, used to transcribe ancient legends, ancestors' triumphs, family trees and anything else that is to be recorded for posterity. For these groups, clothing and adornments serve as an ever-expanding encyclopaedia, to be carried on their person at all times.

In community life, clothing and adornments can serve as an illustrative social code, dictating the roles of gender, age, ethnicity and social status, and defining the division of labour. Clothes and accessories also encompass beliefs relating to folk religion, taboo and fate, spirits and ghosts. From the style, colouring, printing, dyeing and weaving patterns of an ethnic group's dress, we can trace the accumulation of traditional culture. And the way in which ethnic clothing and adornments are passed down through generations represents an important resource in the study of intangible cultural heritage.

Introduction

Above: Miao child's clothing. Rongjiang County, Guizhou.
Photo: Du Dianwen

Right: In the past, twins were seen as the mythical Siblings of the Flood. As such, they couldn't be brought up in society and had to be 'sent back'. This concept no longer stands, and this picture shows twin siblings with the uncle raising them. Jinuo Mountain, Yunnan, 1993

Whether rich or poor, noble or common, of outstanding or contemptible character, all people enter and leave this world in a similar way. Adornments assume particular significance during the major rites of passage in the course of life: birth, coming of age, courtship, marriage and death. This may even continue beyond the final stage; depending on one's beliefs, death heralds the start of the long journey of reincarnation, or a crucible of nothingness.

This book begins with the first adornments of infancy and goes on to observe how the clothing and accessories of various ethnic groups in China embody cultural traditions, and how they are used in ritual practices. In many cultures, the very first ritual surrounding a new life is related to clothing and adornment, intended to protect a vulnerable newborn from physical and spiritual harm. Soon after entering the world, a child is wrapped in clothing symbolic of the culture that will affect – even determine – the shape their life will take.

Later, the various roles they will play in life are visualised through clothing. In ancient times, the Han marked coming of age with a 'capping and pinning' ceremony, in which special adjustments to the hair and headwear signified that a member of society was ready to take on the responsibility of a young adult. And almost every culture has its own take on marriage attire, which honours the legacy of past generations while bringing good fortune to the newlyweds in the future.

Bearing and raising children marks the continuation of the family line, and many ethnic groups have unique clothing customs for this occasion. When children grow up and their parents become grandparents, many cultures offer these elders symbolic clothing, featuring auspicious patterns, shapes and colours, to ensure health and happiness.

Funerals celebrate the soul of the deceased, who has now completed the life cycle and can return to heaven and be reunited with the ancestors. There is a long history of mourning garments in China: among the Han, ancient mourning attire was divided into five 'grades' corresponding to varying degrees of kinship, with strict regulations on the material, shape and appropriate occasion for each.

The importance of family – the central institution in Chinese society – is a thread that runs through these various traditional adornments. Clothing and accessories for each stage of life symbolise cultural belonging, as well as each individual's responsibilities to the family and community: to grow into an upstanding adult, to marry and have children, to honour the ancestors, and to live a life worthy of being mourned upon one's own death.

Since the 1980s, there has been a renewed focus on the value of traditional culture in China. New policies aimed at protecting cultural heritage have brought attention to the diversity of China's ethnic groups and their customs. Yet traditional ways of life are still under threat. Han culture remains dominant. Globalisation, too, is unrelenting; Indigenous people and ethnic minorities all over the world are being forced to abandon tradition in favour of economic survival. For some Chinese ethnic minority groups, the last living gatekeepers of traditional ways are not long for this world.

Even in places where traditional adornments appear to persist, handmade garments have been replaced with wholesale versions. Tourist hotspots around the country are awash with pseudo-folk artefacts and accessories. The sound of a mother's needle, painstakingly stitching a garment for her child with love and compassion, has been drowned out by the roar of production-line machines.

In this context, keeping a record of traditional customs and their original meanings takes on added significance. My research over the last three decades has spanned numerous ethnic minority communities in China's south, north and west; even just in the last decade, many of these communities have changed beyond recognition. Still, in some remote villages of China's borderlands, ethnic dress and accessories prevail. During festivals that mark life's rites of passage, from cradle to grave, traditional outfits – neatly pressed and carefully stored at the bottom of the wardrobe – are donned with pride. The elders maintain that if these clothes are discarded, the ancestors will no longer recognise their living descendants. In mainstream society, too, more and more people are growing tired of the standardised products of the assembly line and feel a deeper connection to clothes and accessories imbued with layers of cultural meaning.

We are all born with an innate love of beauty. But only when we learn to respect and treasure the cultures and values of others, and not simply our own, will we truly live in a world of harmony and colour.

— Professor Deng Qiyao
Guangzhou, September 2020

Dong child's hat, headband and adornments.
Qiandongnan Miao and Dong Autonomous Prefecture, Guizhou, 2014.
Photo: Liu Mingchu

Introduction

Top to bottom, left to right: Hani Aini child's headwear. Xishuangbanna Dai Autonomous Prefecture, Yunnan, 2002; Red cloth basket used to carry children. Banji Village, Hunan, 2013. Photo: Deng Qirong; The lives of those Mongols who survived the fall of the Yuan Dynasty in Yunnan were saved by their armour. These chest ornaments for young children symbolise the protection of their lives and souls. Xingmeng Township, Yunnan, 1991; Yao child's headwear. Liannan Yao Autonomous County, Guangdong, 2004; Tibetan child's ornaments. Qinghai, 2006. Photo: Deng Yuanye; This Naxi girl has a protective seven-star decoration (partially visible) draped across her back. Lijiang, Yunnan, 2006. Photo: Deng Yuanye; Wa girl with chokers and necklaces. Cangyuan Wa Autonomous County, Yunnan, 2004. Photo: Liu Jianming

14

Top to bottom, left to right: Peacock-feather headdress of the Jingpo people. Dehong Dai and Jingpo Autonomous Prefecture, Yunnan, 1993; Rainbow headscarf of a Yi Sani young woman. Shilin Yi Autonomous County, Yunnan, 1997. Photo: Deng Qiyao and Liu Jianming; Jino girl. Jinuo Mountain, Yunnan. Photo: Wang Yizhong; Yi women playing the *zouxiangmie* (a type of mouth harp), which can express a multitude of meanings. The harp box is exquisitely made, and may be a special accessory for a young woman. Shilin Yi Autonomous County, Yunnan. Photo: Liu Jianming; Rainbow headscarf of a Yi Sani young woman. Shilin Yi Autonomous County, Yunnan, 2000. Photo: Liu Jianming; Yi woman's cockscomb hat. Honghe County, Yunnan, 1994; An elderly Yao woman. Guangxi, 2006

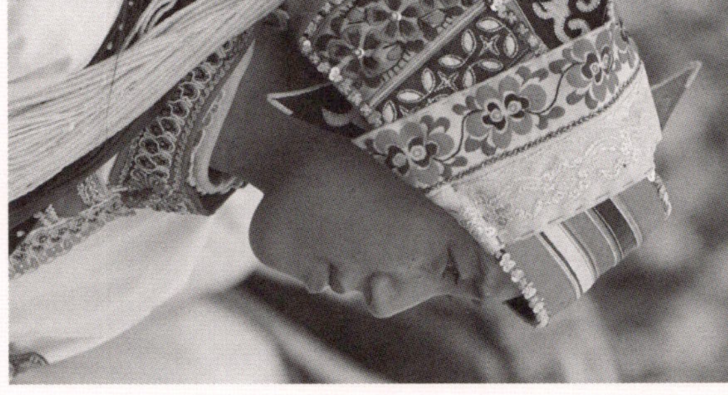

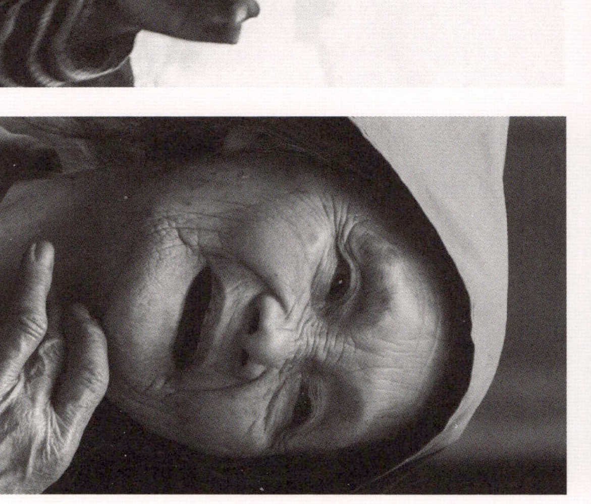

Previous: The Bailuo Yi people,
a branch of the Yi living in Xinzhai
Township, decorate their festival
dress with intricate batik designs.
Chengzhai Village, Wenshan
Zhuang and Miao Autonomous
Prefecture, Yunnan.

Opposite: A traditional Dai wedding
dress in Mandan Village, Dehong
Dai and Jingpo Autonomous
Prefecture, Yunnan Province.

Previous: Bailuo Yi women in hand-embroidered traditional dress at a festival in Chengzhai Village, Yunnan.

Opposite: A Kham Tibetan woman with coral and turquoise accessories attending Losar, a festival to mark the Tibetan new year, at Dzongsar Monastery in Dege County, Garze Tibetan Autonomous Prefecture, Sichuan.

A Kham Tibetan woman holding a
bucket of fresh yak milk on a −20°C
morning in Hongkor, Qinghai. Her
long coat, or *chuba*, is worn with
one arm out of the sleeve – the
'fighting arm' – while the empty
sleeve can hang loose, tuck into
a belt or be used to secure a baby
to her back.

Previous: A view across the
mountains from Basha Village,
Qiandongnan Miao and Dong
Autonomous Prefecture, Guizhou.

This spread: A Kham Tibetan
woman wearing coral and
turquoise for Losar, in Dege
County, Garze Tibetan
Autonomous Prefecture, Sichuan.

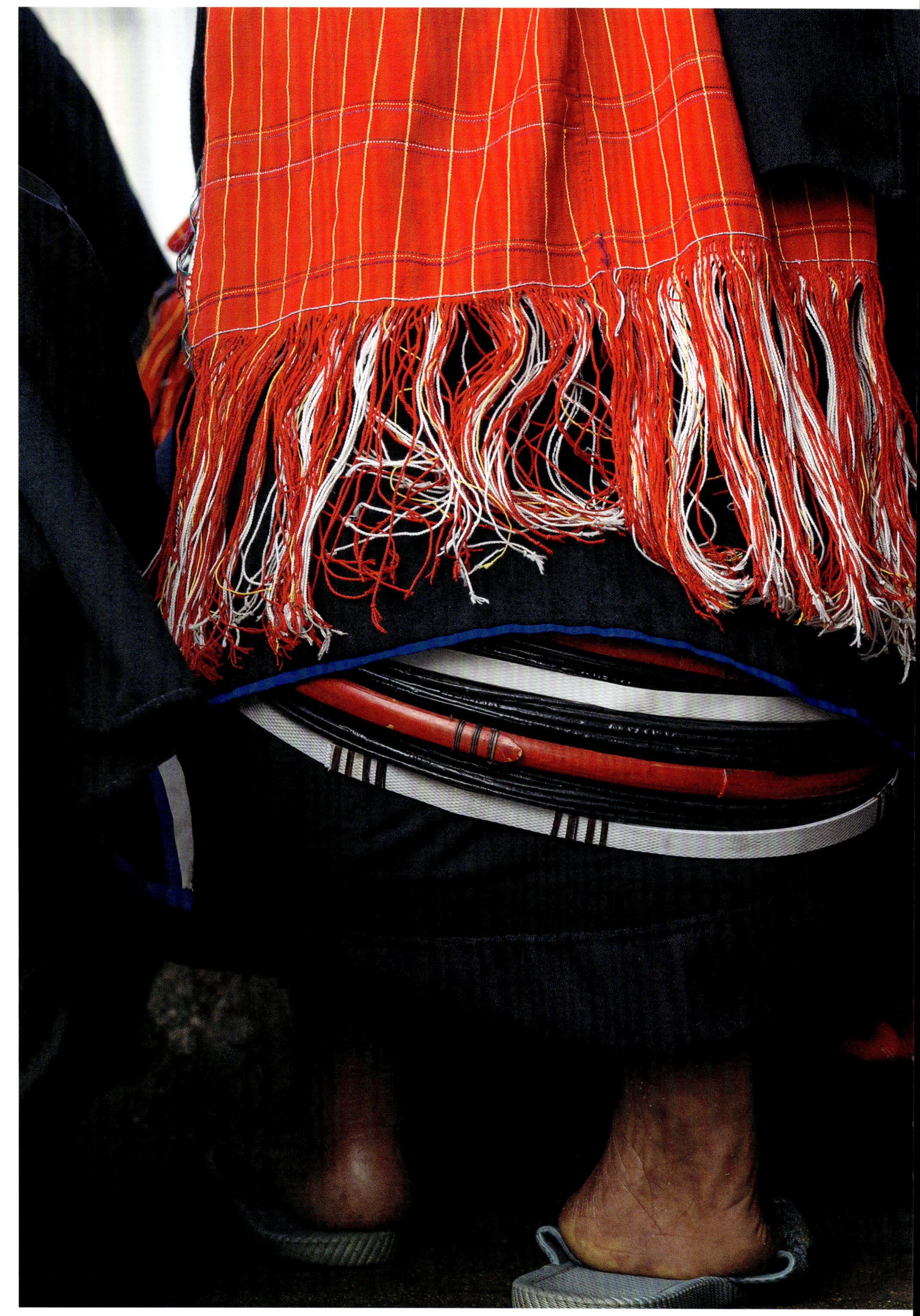

Previous: De'ang women wearing rattan hoops around their waists, indicating that they are married. Padangba Village, Dehong Dai and Jingpo Autonomous Prefecture, Yunnan.

Opposite: A Miao woman from Baibei Village planting rice high up in the Moon Mountain region, Qiandongnan Miao and Dong Autonomous Prefecture, Guizhou. Life in the village revolves around the rice-growing cycle.

The Jiabang rice terraces in Dangniu Village, Qiandongnan Miao and Dong Autonomous Prefecture, Guizhou.

A Flowery Yi woman in traditional dress, clearing the field for new crops in Daping Village, Wenshan Zhuang and Miao Autonomous Prefecture, Yunnan.

Previous left: Kham Tibetan women in Sichuan wear precious stones, amber from Yunnan and red coral that made its way to the Tibetan Plateau via historic trade routes.

Previous right: Amdo Tibetan festival dress in Maqen County, Golog Tibetan Autonomous Prefecture, Qinghai.

This page: Bailuo Yi festival attire, Chengzhai Village, Yunnan.

Opposite: A Hani woman at Sheng Village market in Yuanyang County, Yunnan.

Opposite: Mountains in Getu River National Park, Ziyun Miao and Buyei Autonomous County, Guizhou.

Following left: A traditional Dai wedding dress in Mandan Village, Dehong Dai and Jingpo Autonomous Prefecture, Yunnan.

Following right: A Kham Tibetan woman wearing a traditional *chuba* coat, with yak bone ornaments in her long hair, in Hongkor, Bayan Har Mountains, Qinghai Province.

An Amdo Tibetan woman in festival dress, high up in the Anye Maqen mountains, Qinghai.

Blessed Beginnings

01

Top to bottom, left to right: Hani child's hat. Donglan County, Guangxi, 2007. Photo: Liang Hanchang; Zhuang woman carrying a child and harvesting rice. Photo: Xu Jinyan; Landian Yao child's hat decorated with copper coins, copper bells, beads and red tassels. Tianlin County, Guangxi, 2007. Photo: Liang Hanchang; Miao boy's hat decorated with red tassels and embroidery. Jinping Miao-Yao-Dai Autonomous County, Yunnan, 1991; Miao child with decorative headdress. Rongjiang County, Guizhou. Photo: Du Dianwen; Miao boy with a red belt and a wisp of hair signifying where his soul is supposed to rest. Leishan County, Guizhou, 2006; Hani child in traditional dress. Yuanyang County, Yunnan, 2005. Photo: Liu Jianming; Landian Yao child in a rice paddy wearing a hat decorated with red tassels, beads and silver. Xilin County, Guangxi, 2007. Photo: Liang Hanchang; Pan Yao child's headwear with red tassels that symbolise good luck. Jinxiu County, Guangxi, 2009. Photo: Liang Hanchang

Blessed Beginnings

When I was little, I asked my mother where I came from. 'Naughty children like you are kicked into the world by Yama,' she said teasingly, referring to the god of death. 'Don't believe me? Take a look at the babies born with purple marks on their bottoms! To stop babies going back and causing trouble in the spirit world, as soon as they are born, they are "tied" to the mortal world with string or a symbolic silver lock to ensure they live a long life. We grown-ups have to look out for you.'

Ancient Chinese mythology has it that humanity was created by deities, and babies are the reincarnation of ancestral or other spirits. The realm they come from is in turmoil, a place where spirits wander at will, and they must be physically kicked out to ensure their departure. The spirit of a newborn child is still in a state of unrest, so persistent efforts must be made to secure its place in this world. Among the many ethnic groups who adhere to this belief, adornments connected to birth and infancy rituals take the form of shackles tying the child's soul to the mortal realm.

Shackles, locks and string are not the only way to secure a child's life. Another method is to embellish their clothing, hats, infant wraps, carriers and adornments with auspicious symbols. These serve as charms that can attract good fortune and ward off evil. Baby bonnets and children's headdresses often feature animal imagery: tiger motifs have the power to ward off evil and dogs can prevent bad luck, while dragons symbolise majesty and luxury. As mythical animals, the phoenix and *qilin* (dubbed the 'Chinese unicorn' in the West) are thought to bring good fortune to the family. To enhance the power of such headwear, families will also decorate them with feathers, animal teeth and claws, shells, scented sachets, silver chains and coins. Nothing seems to be off the table.

Compared to most Chinese people of our generation, my wife and I married quite late and had our daughter when we were both past thirty. She was the 'pearl in our palm', we used to say. But becoming parents during the early years of China's one-child policy, as we did, we worried constantly that something might happen to our baby girl. As a comfort, our families taught us how to use the old clothes of family elders to make animal-themed headdresses, adorned with copper coins and dog's teeth, to help protect our child and ward off evil spirits.

Legends and folklore passed from generation to generation inform the adornments that Chinese families bestow upon their children to keep them close and safe. These adornments express various belief systems, blessings of the ancestors and lessons to the young. They can be as simple as a single thread or as complicated as an intricate knot of gold, silver and jade, but their role is always to ensure the healthy growth of children.

Tibetan children's adornments.
Qinghai, 2006. Photo: Deng Yuanye

Top and middle left: Mongolian children's adornments. Tekes County, Xinjiang, 2014

Middle right and bottom: Tibetan children's adornments. Qinghai, 2006. Photo: Deng Yuanye

Top to bottom, left to right: Hani child with toad pattern embroidery. Jinping County, Yunnan, 1993; Bai baby carrier. Dali, Yunnan, 2007. Photo: Liu Jianming; The white tassels of Hani children's headwear symbolise respect for elders who have passed away. Jinping County, Yunnan, 1991; Hani child's headwear. Honghe, Yunnan, 2007. Photo: Liu Jianming; The owl eyes depicted on the headwear of Hani children are supposed to ward off evil spirits. Jinping County, Yunnan, 1991

Blessed Beginnings

Souls at Stake

Jino folklore states that a person is born into this world with the gourd's help, and therefore the placenta should be placed in a gourd as a means of communicating with the gods.

—

Jino infant hats are adorned with shells, dog bones and small pieces of iron, to protect the baby's soul and help it settle into its new world.

In January 1993, I visited southern Yunnan Province with a film crew to make a documentary about the customs of the Jino ethnic group. Jino people live in the Mekong river basin and number around 20,000. Although I had already carried out almost a decade of anthropological research on communities in Yunnan, this would be my first visit to a Jino village, and I was all the more excited for it. A little over 50 kilometres east of Jinghong, the capital of Xishuangbanna Dai Autonomous Prefecture, we left the flatlands behind and made our way up a cobblestoned mountain path. Before long, we had reached Jinuo Mountain. Although it was the middle of winter, there was a spring warmth in the air. Buildings of golden bamboo drifted in and out of view as we trekked through the lush rainforest and broad-leaved evergreens.

Upon entering the village, we heard an agonised groan coming from a group of bamboo huts enclosed by a fence. We rushed into the central courtyard, asking if we could help in any way, and soon realised that the sound had come from one of the huts where a woman was in labour.

When Jino babies are born, it is believed that their souls are in danger of floating away. To save the newborn, the father or another patriarch of the family places the placenta in a gourd (the origin of all humankind, according to some creation myths) and buries it under one of the pillars of the house; this symbolises that the child will grow up to be a pillar of support for the family. Over the gourd is placed a bamboo basket, fastened with nine wooden stakes for a boy or seven for a girl, to secure the child's soul.

The numbers seven and nine originate from a Jino creation myth, which holds that before human life was created by a goddess named Pimo, spirits wandered aimlessly in the abyss between the earth and the sky. To enter the human world, these spirits needed souls — nine to become a man, seven to become a woman. Seven and nine permeate many aspects of Jino culture and adornment: at birth, alongside the gourd ritual, either seven or nine pieces of ginger are hung from both the mother's neck and the baby's hat using white thread. Later, as adults, Jino men wear nine stripes on the lapels and cuffs of their clothing, while women wear seven.

Just as we were about to leave the courtyard, the sister of the woman who was giving birth pointed out a bamboo X-shape hanging over the gateway. Laughing, she said, 'Didn't you notice that? It is a mark to warn outsiders not to come in. Since you entered the maternal home, you've violated a taboo! According to our custom, seven days after the birth, you must all come back, and one of you must become the child's godfather.' Only after seven days, when the newborn's umbilical cord has fallen off, can he or she be greeted by people outside the family. To comply with the custom, on the seventh day we returned to the bamboo hut bearing gifts. As the eldest of our documentary crew, the director was duly named godfather.

Nine days after a baby is born, a ritual called *asanmu* is held, whereby the parents tie a red knot onto the baby's hat. This harnesses the spirit of a newborn and is the first accessory a child receives. The parents choose a spiritual name for the baby based on the name of the shaman presiding over the ceremony. This is also to ensure the baby's soul settles into the world, and that the gods will bless them, ensuring that they will be healthy and prosperous as their life unfolds.

Hani Aini child's hat adorned with silver coins, copper coins and silver chains. Xishuangbanna, Yunnan, 2002

Above: The uncle of a newborn buries the baby's placenta under a pillar of their house and covers the area with a bamboo basket. Xishuangbanna, Yunnan, 1993

Body and Soul

Among many ethnic groups, it is traditionally believed that the hair, nails and placenta are intimately linked with a person's safety and fate. Along with the body, they are considered an inheritance from one's parents to be treated with great care. *Fa*, *xu*, *zhua* – hair, beard, nails – is an important theme in Chinese folklore, and the treatment of the placenta is a key part of many birth ceremonies in China. For example, after the Blang women of Yunnan's Xishuangbanna Dai Autonomous Prefecture give birth, a small section of the umbilical cord is cut, wrapped in a small white cloth, and placed under the baby's bonnet.

The Yi people of Liangshan Yi Autonomous Prefecture, in Sichuan Province, choose an auspicious day sometime between three days and a month after a child's birth. At sunrise, they hold a hair-cutting ceremony in the courtyard. They sew new clothes for the child and use a piece of cloth from the collar to make a small bag, which holds the cut locks of hair. The bag is then tied to the child's clothes or the corner of their hat.

—

There are dozens of different types of traditional Chinese decorative knots, many of them intricate in both form and meaning. For example, the Double Connection Knot symbolises many years of surplus and success; the Double Line Knot – also known as the Money Knot or the Double Coin Knot – resembles two interwoven coins, symbolising that good things come in pairs. Butterfly Knots are adorned with copper coins as blessings, while the Double Butterfly symbolises two hearts beating as one. And the elaborate Panchang Knot has an endless loop that connotes mutual dependence, endurance and longevity.

—

Combinations of knots can also represent phrases. For example, the ji, qing and yu knots together mean jiqing youyu, or 'many happy things'. Sewing aromatic material into a cloth bag turns it into a scented sachet, and, with corresponding knots, it becomes a beautiful accessory permeated with cultural meaning.

Elders tie a red egg with coloured thread and hang it from a baby participating in the *man yue* wine ceremony for good luck. **Guangxi, 2003. Photo: Liang Hanchang**

Top row: Sending baby carriers to friends and relatives who have given birth is one of the Yao fertility customs. Bama County, Guangxi, 2008. Photo: Liang Hanchang

Middle rows to bottom, left to right: Bai girls fishing. Dali, Yunnan, 2009; A Zhuang mother carrying her child on her back travels to the city to sell vegetables. Rongshui County, Guangxi, 2010. Photo: Liang Hanchang; A young Dai mother and her son, dressed in new clothes. Jiangcheng County, Yunnan, 2009; Nu woman with baby carrier. Gongshan County, Yunnan, 2004. Photo: Liu Jianming; For annual holidays and festivities, Yao mothers must dress their children as finely as themselves. Nandan County, Guangxi, 2010. Photo: Liang Hanchang; Baiku Yao child's hat adorned with a Panwang pattern, symbolising protection received from the ancestor spirits. Nandan County, Guangxi, 2009. Photo: Liang Hanchang

Above, top to bottom: Zhuang embroidered baby carrier.
Leye County, Guangxi, 2008. Photo: Liang Hanchang; Zhuang flower-
embroidered and brocade baby carrier. **Huanjiang County,
Guangxi, 2008. Photo: Liang Hanchang**

Right: Baiku Yao child's Panwang pattern embroidery.
Nandan County, Guangxi, 2009

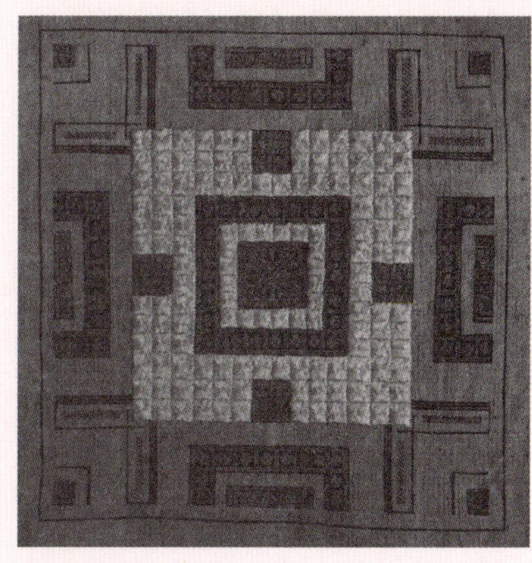

   Blessed Beginnings

The Power of Precious Metals

Many ethnic groups in China share the custom of adorning infants with silver collars or wrist and ankle bracelets. This is said to 'seal' the most vulnerable parts of the body, preventing the child's soul from escaping. Frail children are in particular need of protection, to ensure their wandering souls are locked in – and not in danger of escaping or being overrun by wild spirits – so that they can live a long and healthy life.

These ornaments are often engraved with images of dragons, phoenixes, *qilin*, fish, butterflies and other creatures that are considered auspicious, and are meant to accompany children throughout their lives. Along with the development of both material and spiritual culture, many of the silver chains and locks have gradually evolved into light and beautiful bracelets, cuffs and necklaces.

The Miao are one of the groups that believe in the protective power of silver. Historically a migratory people, the Miao would use their silver ornaments to ascertain if there was any poison in the water or soil when they moved to new land. If either was poisonous, the silver would turn black. Evil spirits are considered a supernatural form of poison that only silver can counteract, so adorning children with silver is believed to drive away malevolent spirits.

—

Copper and silver in particular are thought to exorcise evil spirits. The Dai people believe that if you wear copper (or, better still, gold or silver), ghosts and evil spirits will not come near you.

—

During Miao festivals, parents adorn their children with silver crowns, chains, collars, bracelets and other ornaments. As they grow, children are covered in more and more silver, since the Miao believe it can detect poison and deter evil spirits.

Fan Yao girls covered with protective silver locks, collars, necklaces, bells and pendants – accessories that will accompany them throughout their lives. **Bama County, Guangxi, 2007. Photo: Liang Hanchang**

Miao silver–horned headdress. Qiandongnan, Guizhou, 2015

Miao girls and young women in silver headdresses, collars and locks. Qiandongnan, Guizhou, 2006. Photo: Deng Yuanye

Miao girl with silver crown, collar and lock.
Qiandongnan, Guizhou, 2006. Photo: Deng Yuanye

Adornments for Dong girls.
Liping County, Guizhou. Photo:
Wu Dongjun

Dong children wearing
symbolic locks and chains.
Liping County, Guizhou. Photo:
Yang Xingbin

Longevity Locks

—

The Xiong Can ceremony is held on a Day of the Sheep, according to the twelve-day zodiac cycle that some groups observe. Chickens and pigs are killed for a big feast. The priest instructs the host to prepare a wooden container of rice with twelve red eggs inside. The child, the child's uncle and the priest get two red eggs each, while the remaining six eggs are given to attending relatives and friends.

—

During the Xiong Can ceremony, a piece of cloth from the child's clothing is wrapped together with a piece of red cloth, and then twelve miniature figures are cut out of this fabric and tied to a wooden stool, in what is known as 'hanging red'.

While researching in the south-western province of Guizhou in 2006, I asked a Miao woman why local children often wore large metal chains around their necks. She explained that these are longevity locks, which elders say can protect the child against evil spirits. They are given to a child after their *man yue*, or one-month birthday, during a ceremony called Xiong Can.

Silver is of utmost importance in Xiong Can; all guests at the ceremony must donate money towards the crafting of silver adornments the child will wear as symbols of luck and longevity. At the end of the ceremony, the priest places a silver necklace around the child's neck – this longevity lock will have been consecrated at the ancestral altar, then steeped in alcohol and 'contact blessed' by three fish freshly caught and prepared that day. The necklace will then bring the child enough food to eat and clothes to wear throughout the year, keep them away from harm, give them much happiness and grant them longevity.

A silver pendant engraved with the image of the child's zodiac sign is also given to the child. Young girls are sometimes similarly gifted silver 'life-saving' bracelets that have been blessed. These accessories are designed to protect a child and must be worn for a lifetime.

The Miao and other ethnic groups, including Mongolian communities in Yunnan, also hold a ceremony whereby a mother and child have to pass through 100 symbolic gateways before being tied together with an iron chain, secured with a lock. With this adornment hanging round them, mother and child must return to their home and pass through a burning bail of straw, before unlocking the lock to complete the ceremony and protect the child from harm.

Top: Miao girl with silver crown, collar and lock. Qiandongnan, Guizhou, 2006. Photo: Deng Yuanye

Bottom: Miao child's silver lock. Leishan, Guizhou, 2006. Photo: Deng Yuanye; Bailuo Yi girl with festival adornments. Wenshan, Yunnan, 2018. Photo: Cat Vinton

Top: Miao girls with silver crowns, collars and locks. Qiandongnan, Guizhou, 2006. Photo: Deng Yuanye

Bottom: Bailuo Yi girls wearing festival headdresses. Wenshan, Yunnan, 2018. Photo: Cat Vinton

Tiger and Rooster Headdresses

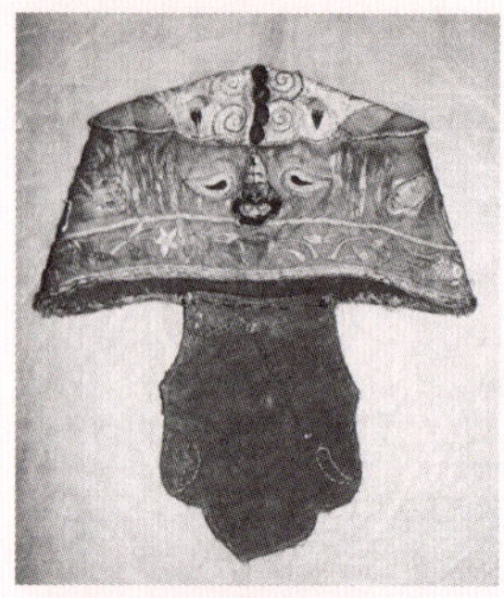

Miao tiger-themed headwear. **Kaili, Guizhou, 2006**

In the summer of 1988, I was conducting field work in the mountains of central Yunnan, observing the clothing of the Yi people. On entering a Yi village, I saw a group of older women dressed in cyan-embroidered clothing. They were doing needlework in front of a dry-brick house built of red clay, and there were many children playing around them. The boys were wearing tiger-themed headdresses adorned with shells, silver chains and red tassels. One of the women told me that the Yi are descended from a tiger, and wear tiger headdresses so that the ancestors will bless and protect their descendants.

The girls' accessories were even more dazzling. Their hats were shaped like a rooster's comb, with large red flower buds embroidered on the front, and images of roosters, flowers and birds on both sides. A design resembling the auspicious Chinese character 米 ('rice') decorated the top, which was further adorned with silver chains, and silver and copper coins. The woman explained that girls' souls are mostly *yin* – in contrast to the opposing *yang* life force associated with masculinity – and need the heavily *yang* rooster hat to achieve harmony.

The Yi have a population of nearly 9 million, spread out across the vast mountains of south-western China. Their clothing and adornments have certain commonalities, but there are hundreds of variations between different branches and villages. In the spring of 1990, I visited a different branch of the Yi to take part in their traditional Saizhuang Festival – literally the 'clothing-competing festival'.

As soon as we entered the village, a group of children encircled us, wide-eyed at the rare sight of city-folk. A boy of no more than three or four years old stared intently at the camera I held in my hands. His tiger headdress was embroidered with many beautiful and auspicious patterns. Its front was inlaid with images of five gods (each representing a cardinal direction, plus the centre); its sides were decorated with animal teeth hanging from red threads; and its brim was embellished with beads and colourful tassels. Another child, younger still, wore a round hat with a hole in the top. The child's mother told me that the small hole was a 'skylight' made so that the gods could keep an eye on the child's soul.

In addition to traditional shells and flowers, the hat was also adorned with an animal claw. The mother explained that their community's elders believed that when Bima Wen (the Monkey King from the classic Ming Dynasty novel *Journey to the West*) looked after horses, they never got sick; so, if a child falls ill easily, attaching a monkey's finger to their headdress can offer protection.

Above, left to right: Zhuang child's swallowtail hat decorated with silver. Maguan County, Yunnan, 2009. Photo: Liang Hanchang; Religious and auspicious patterns on a Miao child's hat. Kaili, Guizhou, 2006

Left, top to bottom: Bai cockscomb hat. Dali, Yunnan, 2006. Photo: Liu Jianming; Dai child's hat. Yunnan Provincial Museum, Kunming, Yunnan

Right: Bai child's phoenix hat. Dali, Yunnan, 2018

Top and middle left: Kazakh children's feathered hats. Tekes County, Xinjiang, 2014

Middle right: Dai girl's headdress. Dehong, Yunnan, 2018

Bottom: The animal teeth used on Yao children's hats ward off evil spirits. Jinping County, Yunnan, 1993

Flowers and Feathers

—

Scented sachets may be filled with medicinal herbs such as peppermint, clove, costus, Chinese angelica, valerian, wild ginger, ginseng, Chinese liquorice, forsythia, mugwort and patchouli, in order to repel mosquitoes and prevent colds.

—

Solidified plant secretions can also become valuable adornments, as in the use of amber (fossilised tree resin) in Tibetan jewellery.

The custom of wearing animal bones and teeth, bird feathers and claws, can be traced back to traditional hunter-gatherer lifestyles, but these relics have since taken on additional spiritual significance. For example, the floral-themed caps worn by children in the Yao village of Tailing, in southern Yunnan, are ornamented with an animal tooth carefully decorated with coloured thread, designed to drive away evil spirits and protect the child's soul.

Plants are often used as accessories for their beauty, aroma and availability, and are usually a favourite among young girls. Ethnic groups from mountainous regions often use vines to bind wildflowers together into a garland for a child's headdress. Plants with a beautiful appearance and fragrance may be used as ornaments to symbolise good fortune, while some strongly scented plants can serve the dual purposes of warding off both mosquitoes and evil spirits. A child might see merely a pretty flower, but parents and grandparents are aware of its spiritual significance and the continuation of a tradition passed down from their ancestors.

As protective adornments for their child's hat or body, Yi people use grass and star anise, the Jino people ginger slices, the Hani garlic and *hongpao* (hill raspberry) leaves. The Wa worship the *hongmao* (rambutan) tree and believe that wearing its leaves can provide protection from the spirits. And in Xishuangbanna, in the mountainous villages where the Aini branch of the Hani ethnic group reside, all children's headwear must be adorned with red feathers. The Hani Aini consider red to be the colour of heaven; if the red feather on a child's cap quivers, it is thought to be a sign that the gods are present and so ghosts will not dare intrude.

Hani Aini woman wearing a hat decorated with red pompoms and metal ornaments. The small cloth bag hung from the child's arm contains objects to ward off evil spirits. **Xishuangbanna, Yunnan, 2010. Photo: Liu Jianming**

The Legend of the Golden Temple

In the summer of 1991, I returned to the ethnic Mongolian village of Tonghai, in Yunnan, for the first time in eleven years. Most people think of Mongolians as nomadic, sleeping in yurts and sweeping across the vast steppes on horseback. However, there is a small Mongolian outpost in southern Yunnan, thousands of miles away from their northern counterparts, which is home to around 5000 ethnic Mongolians. They are fishers, masons and farmers, and are said to be the descendants of soldiers who remained after Kublai Khan's southern campaign in the 13th century.

The Yunnan Mongolians have long since abandoned their traditional yurt homes and constructed brick houses. When I stayed in the village, I would often head down to the area where the elders gathered to chat idly and tell legends of their ancestors. One day, a grandmother passed by, her young grandson in her arms. She had dressed him in traditional clothing, with a silver chain hanging from his neck. His headdress, too, was heavily adorned with silver. When they saw my obvious interest, several of the elders clamoured to tell me the legend behind the silver decorations.

In the latter years of the Yuan Dynasty (1279–1368), a branch of the Mongolian army was defeated in a great battle in Yunnan. Only seven soldiers and seven horses survived. They fled until they reached Qilu Lake, where they faced a vast expanse of water, while serried ranks of enemy soldiers advanced behind, leaving them trapped. Suddenly, a golden bridge appeared on the lake, and they hurried across it to safety. No sooner had they crossed the bridge than it disappeared. But, although they had escaped the pursuing soldiers, they didn't know how to survive and make a life for themselves in this unfamiliar place.

Not long after, an old man standing on a rhinoceros-hide raft emerged from the water. He invited them to join him and guided them to the centre of the lake. There, he pointed out a big fish bearing a golden temple on its back. Safely returned to the shore, the people understood his message: if a fish can sustain a temple, it can sustain us as food (in Chinese, the words for 'temple' and 'food' have similar pronunciations). From then on, they survived by catching fish and shrimp from the lake. To give thanks, the local Mongolians now attach a silver ornament depicting a fish with a temple onto the headdresses of their children, to make sure their saviour is not forgotten by their descendants.

Mongolian child with a headdress honouring the gods who guided their ancestors through difficult times. **Tonghai County, Yunnan, 1991**

To ward off evil spirits, Miao clothing and Yao baby carriers bear ornaments such as *bagua* (eight trigram) silver plates, bat silver jewellery, copper coins, copper bells and red tassels. **Jinxiu County, Guangxi, 2006**

Far bottom right: Hani waistcoat with owl pattern. **Evergrand Art Museum, Taiwan (originally from Honghe, Yunnan), 2006**

Top and middle, left to right: Hani child's hat. Yuanyang County, Yunnan, 2008. Photo: Liu Jianming; Zhuang child's silver adornments. Maguan County, Yunnan, 2008. Photo: Liang Hanchang; Bouyei girl's headwear. Luoping County, Yunnan, 1997; Yao child's hat. Jinxiu County, Guangxi, 2006

Bottom: Hani Nuobi child's waistcoat with owl face pattern on the front. Honghe, Yunnan, 1993

Top, left to right: Hani baby carrier. Honghe, Yunnan, 2008. Photo: Liu Jianming; Hani child's hat. Honghe, Yunnan, 2008. Photo: Liu Jianming

Middle: Hani Aini child's hat decorated with silver coins, copper coins and silver chains. Xishuangbanna, Yunnan, 2002

Bottom, left to right: Dai girl's headwear. Yuanjiang County, Yunnan, 2010; Hani Aini child's hat decorated with silver coins, copper coins and silver chains. Xishuangbanna, Yunnan, 1997. Photo: Xu Ye

Blessed Beginnings

Previous: A Kham Tibetan woman in a *chuba*, a coat traditionally worn with one arm free, holding a child in Dege County, Garze Tibetan Autonomous Prefecture, Sichuan.

Opposite: A young Miao mother collecting water with her baby in Basha Village, Qiandongnan Miao and Dong Autonomous Prefecture, Guizhou.

Opposite: A Miao woman and
baby at Laomeng market,
Honghe Hani and Yi Autonomous
Prefecture, Yunnan.

Following spread: Bailuo Yi girls
wearing handmade batik clothing
and ornate headdresses at a festival
in Chengzhai Village, Wenshan
Zhuang and Miao Autonomous
Prefecture, Yunnan.

A Miao boy from Basha Village, Guizhou.

A Kham Tibetan girl collecting water in Hongkor, Bayan Har Mountains, Qinghai.

This spread: A young Miao boy from Basha Village, Guizhou, sporting a traditional men's haircut. The style once marked the transition to adulthood around the age of fifteen but is now worn by boys of all ages.

An Amdo Tibetan family
attending Tibetan new year
celebrations at a temple in
Maqen County, Golog Tibetan
Autonomous Prefecture, Qinghai.

A Bailuo Yi girl wearing a
festival headdress in
Chengzhai Village, Yunnan.

An Amdo Tibetan child
dressed for a festival in
Maqen County, Qinghai.

This spread: A Kham Tibetan
mother and child preparing a
family dinner of *thukpa*, a noodle
soup, in Hongkor, Qinghai.

Winter on the Tibetan Plateau,
some 4000 metres above sea level.

Opposite: A Kham Tibetan woman in a *chuba* holding a child in Dege County, Sichuan.

Above: An Amdo Tibetan girl attending Tibetan new year celebrations at a temple in Maqen County, Qinghai.

A Miao girl at Laomeng
market, Yunnan.

Previous: The Basha Miao are among the last hunter-gatherers of China; rifles and hunting knives are important accessories for men and boys. Basha Village, Guizhou.

Below: Sunrise in Dahe Miao Village, a remote Miao community deep within Getu River National Park, Ziyun Miao and Buyei Autonomous County, Guizhou.

Opposite: A Bailuo Yi boy wearing a festival headdress in Chengzhai Village, Yunnan.

A Bailuo Yi child dressed for a
festival in Chengzhai Village, Yunnan.

Pink blossom in the Xinzhai township of Malipo Country, Yunnan.

This spread: Two young Hani
girls prepare for a festival in
Mangjia Village, Xishuangbanna
Dai Autonomous Prefecture,
Yunnan Province.

Kham Tibetan boys wearing traditional
chuba in Dege County, Sichuan.

An abundance of butterflies gather
by the river in Mangjia Village,
Xishuangbanna Dai Autonomous
Prefecture, Yunnan.

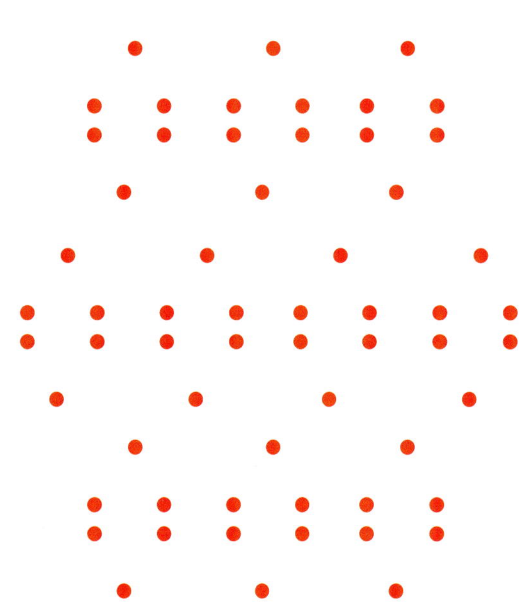

Coming of Age

02

Age

Top to bottom: Young Yao men and women throw flowers at each other in courtship. Wenshan, Yunnan, 1980. Photo: Wang Lili; Guoshan Yao men celebrate coming of age with the *qixingejie* ceremony. Hezhou, Guangxi, 2010. Photo: Liang Hanchang; The music tradition of antiphonal singing is a way for young Yao men and women to express their feelings. Wenshan, Yunnan, 1980. Photo: Wang Lili

Coming of Age

One of the most touching aspects of my research in anthropology concerns the folk culture of coming of age and the ensuing expectations of courtship. Beliefs, customs and taboos among various ethnic groups may differ widely, but people's longing for and pursuit of love is universal.

Just like birds who fan their bright feathers in courtship, young men and women use their clothing and accessories to show the community that they've come of age and are ready to fall in love. The traditional clothing of ethnic minority groups, especially that of young women, is often decorated in a way that indicates their popularity and relationship status – so different from the Han courtship of my youth, when a young couple would merely exchange letters or share a meal.

On one occasion, a young Dai woman saw me staring at her headdress and said disdainfully, 'You Han live very boring lives. I have been to a nearby Han village: it feels so dead during the day – no one sings – and there is no singing and dancing at night either. Nothing happens there! People just live in silence and then they give birth to a bunch of babies.' She wasn't wrong.

My own youth occurred during a time when people sought security in the anonymity of grey and blue clothing. If your clothes revealed the tiniest glimpse of skin, you would be condemned as a hooligan – so you can imagine my shock when I first saw a young Dai woman wearing a fitted short-sleeved top, or a Hani Yiche woman in a blouse that showed her navel. I grew up with a sense of shame about love; after all, most of the romantic films, novels and songs I encountered in 1960s and 70s China were dismissed as 'pornographic', criticised and banned. But later, when my daughter was young, I told her, 'Teenagers must wear beautiful clothes!' Having seen the colourful outfits of groups like the Dai, Jingpo and Hani during the time I spent in rural China, I had come around to believing that young people should fill their days with vibrant attire and the passion of love.

When the youth of any culture enter adolescence, they trade in their childhood clothing for young-adult fashions, as dictated by the custom and styles of their time and place. Many Chinese ethnic groups hold coming-of-age rites to mark this transformation – symbolising through clothing and ritual not just the physical maturation of an individual, but also their growing spiritual and social commitments to the community.

Coming-of-age rites have a long history in China. Among the Han, a set of ceremonies known as the *guanji* rituals were prevalent before the collapse of the Qing Dynasty in 1912. Through the transformation of hairstyles and accessories, these rituals publicly demonstrated that a young person had come of age and would soon be ready to start a family and career. Notably, the day of the ceremony also marked the beginning of parents' discussions about arranged marriages for their children.

Clothing and adornments feature heavily in coming-of-age ceremonies and can reveal important information about the traditions, rules and gender expectations of an ethnic group. Young men often adopt adornments and accessories that embody the traditional masculine ideals of a community: for example, among the Blang in Xishuangbanna Dai Autonomous Prefecture, Yunnan Province, boys of fourteen or fifteen receive a dagger and a traditional reed instrument a *lusheng* to symbolise the bravery and artistry Blang men are expected to exhibit during courtship.

For young women, much of the focus is on sexuality and the bearing and raising of children. In many Chinese ethnic communities, it is not until a young woman crosses the threshold of adulthood through a coming-of-age ritual that she is allowed to become sexually active. Ceremonies symbolise this transition with

Hani teenage girls' adornments.
Honghe, Yunnan, 2005.
Photo: Liu Jianming

special adornments, such as the woollen skirt that is ceremonially draped around a young Yi woman's head and then her thighs by a family matriarch. Young women's adornments are also designed to distinguish them from young girls, shielding the latter from advances by men.

A key purpose of coming-of-age rites for both boys and girls is to gain recognition from the ancestors, who must accept newly minted adults into the hierarchy of the clan. Some groups treat coming of age as a rebirth; merely being born the first time isn't enough to grant them full recognition from their culture's ancestors and gods.

Coming-of-age rites represent the inheritance of traditions and spiritual beliefs by the next generation of adults. It is little surprise, then, that such ceremonies are often held in tandem with a community's largest or most important festivals, occasions that warrant vibrant traditional dress and dazzling accessories. Through coming-of-age ceremonies, communities convey to ancestors and gods that an individual is on the verge of adulthood, and grant recognition from both the land of the living and the land of the spirits.

Young Yi men and women frolicking in the hills. **Chuxiong, Yunnan, 1990**

Top: Dong young women with plain dresses, silver chains, girdles and body adornments. Qiandongnan, Guizhou, 2006. Photo: Deng Yuanye

Bottom, left to right: Yi young women's clothing. Shiping County, Yunnan, 1994; Baima Tibetan girl's outfit. Sichuan, 2006. Photo: Gou Yujuan

Born Again

Liannan County, Guangdong, 2004

The Yao people believe that in order to come of age, boys must gain the approval of their ancestors and wider community through a ritual called *dujie*. This spiritual ceremony is even more important to the Yao than a wedding, as without it the vital link to the ancestors would be severed.

Each branch of the geographically diverse Yao has its own form of *dujie*. Most run in cycles of a few years and are held at the same time as other major ancestral festivals. During the ceremony, boys and young men ranging in age from just over ten to around twenty-four complete rituals symbolising the birth process. In one, the participant ascends a high bamboo platform, curls into a foetal position and is wrapped in a robe or cloth, while the presiding shaman sings prayers to welcome his birth. The boy then rolls off the platform and is caught in a sheet held by the watching crowd. The complex *dujie* ceremonies typically last three days and nights, with the shaman becoming the rebirth parent. By the end, the young men have been given new spritual names, signifying that they are now connected with their ancestors.

Yao coming-of-age rites may vary from region to region, but there are similarities in the associated adornments, which often include headpieces consisting of red or black headbands embroidered with the image of the Yao ancestor Panwang (King Pan) and decorated with metallic ornaments and feathers, and strips of red cloth draped across the chest.

In the winter of 2004, I heard of one such coming-of-age ceremony that was to take place during a grand festival in honour of Panwang. The festival would include the all-important Shua Ge Tang ceremony, a Yao gathering of dancing and singing that honours forebears, celebrates the harvest and informs the ancestors through *dujie* rituals that the male children of the family have come of age. It seemed an opportunity not to be missed – especially because the ceremony had been banned for almost fifty years, a casualty of China's turbulent politics.

My wife and I travelled for a day to reach a Yao village outside Qingyuan, in Guangdong Province. The village was accessible only via a rugged mountain path, and we endured an hour of biting cold and winding mountain tracks before finally arriving at the home of our Yao host shortly before nightfall.

The house was perched on the side of a mountain, and it had wooden walls and a roof made of bark. In the upstairs living room, an altar to the Yao gods stood opposite the door. We all sat around the firepit in the centre, talking about the upcoming Shua Ge Tang ceremony. Our host was the fifty-year-old son of a local dignitary; his father would ordinarily have presided over the ceremony but, at more than eighty years of age, he had decided to pass on this responsibility to his son and several other middle-aged locals.

Our host – who, like most in the village, had the surname Fang – told us that the village elders were concerned by the long interval since the last ceremony. They feared that if they were unable to worship the ancestors at Shua Ge Tang, the ghosts of the ancestors would come back to life and wreak havoc, damaging their family's health and disrupting their affairs. Therefore, our host explained, at this long-awaited Shua Ge Tang ceremony, every male member of the Fang family without a spiritual name had to participate in the *dujie* ritual. He spoke slowly, the excitement and tension evident in his face. What I really wanted to know but didn't dare ask was whether those who had died without ever receiving a spiritual name would be accepted by the ancestors. Later, I learned that this was a taboo question, and it remains unanswered.

The following day, proceedings began with the naming ceremony. Those taking part were supposed to have abstained from killing animals, eating meat, swearing and having sex for anywhere between one and five days beforehand. Under the watchful eye of the presiding dignitaries, villagers wearing traditional dress and feathered headdresses beat drums as they ascended the mountain to summon the ancestral spirits. This was followed by worship and prayer, the blowing of a bullhorn, burning paper money and sacrificing a chicken, all for the purpose of gaining recognition from the ancestors and gods. Acting as priests, the dignitaries wore red headbands and headpieces embellished with silver ornaments depicting the gods, or headgear fashioned from horsehair. Their red tunics and long gowns were also embroidered with imagery of gods and spirits.

When the time came, they wrote spritual names on slips of paper and scattered them among the *dujie* participants. Each vied for a slip and adopted whatever name was written on it. The dignitaries then inscribed these names on headdresses decorated with images of the gods, and the villagers dressed the newly initiated young men in beautiful clothes, accessorised with earrings, necklaces and bracelets adorned with feathers – a nod to their ancestors' hunting prowess.

The *dujie* rituals continued for three days, intertwined with ancestor-worship ceremonies that celebrated the Yao ancestors' arduous migration across the nine regions of ancient China. During these ceremonies, relatives placed red ribbons and other colourful accessories on those who had just taken a spiritual name. By the end, Fang men of all ages had officially come of age in the eyes of the ancestors.

Liannan County, Guangdong, 2004

—
Although the dujie *ceremony is only for young men, it is the grandest celebration in the Yao calendar, so women and children will also dress up to worship the gods and ancestors, and pray for the family's future wellbeing.*

Coming of Age

Top three rows: Yao 'nine regions' ceremonies. Liannan County, Guangdong, 2004/2005

Bottom, left to right: Daoist priests chant prayers during the Yao *dujie* (coming-of-age) ceremony. Photo: Zhang Yuan; During one Yao *dujie* ritual to symbolise rebirth, a participant sits on top of a high platform with a sacred crown on his head, before rolling into a piece of cloth held by the crowd below. Wenshan, Yunnan, 2007. Photo: Wang Mingfu

Top to bottom, left to right: Yao women's clothing. Liannan County, Guangdong, 2004; Yao youths sing folk songs after their coming-of-age ceremony. Jinxiu County, Guangxi, 2007. Photo: Liang Hanchang; Yao youths participate in a naming ceremony. Liannan County, Guangdong, 2004

Silver Snails and Knotted Waistbands

The Yiche branch of the Hani people live on the southern side of the Honghe, or Red River, in Yunnan. Unlike the elaborate dress of Aini women, Yiche women's attire is simple and minimal, allowing them to work in the terraced rice paddies and traverse the muddy banks with ease. In 1986 and 1993, I was involved in two ethnographic documentary projects about the Yiche people – and, to this day, I still remember how shocked I was when I first saw them dressed in shorts and revealing tops. Nowadays, most young people only wear traditional clothes during festivals, but they remain an important part of Yiche heritage and are imbued with intricate layers of meaning.

Yiche custom dictates that once a young woman reaches dating age, her parents will build her a small apartment attached to the main house, to give her the space and privacy to receive men. At the same time, women begin wearing the traditional *quepa* undergarment, *quema* shirt and *quelang* jacket, sharp-pointed white headdress, *laba* shorts and waistband.

The four thin strands of the waistband have a mythical significance: in ancient times, when heaven and earth were in chaos and *yin* and *yang* were out of balance, one of the gods used four strands of rope to fasten together the four corners of the heavens, and only then was everything restored to harmony. The waistband of each Yiche woman has its own unique, intricate method of fastening, which supposedly only her *cheai* (lover) knows how to untie. Hanging from the waistband are silver ornaments shaped like fish and snails. These ornaments symbolise fertility and are linked to Hani mythology, which speaks of an age when mighty floods destroyed the world, and the gods made humans seek the seeds of new life in the belly of a fish.

The traditional blouse worn by young Yiche women has a collarless front, with seventeen decorative buckles sewn onto the left side. The hem has a curved opening like a turtle's shell (hence the name 'turtle blouse'), which would be left unfastened in the past to partially expose the right breast – touching the breast was a means of greeting between lovers.

Above and right: Hani Yiche waist decorations feature silver snails. **Honghe County, 2007. Photo: Liu Jianming**

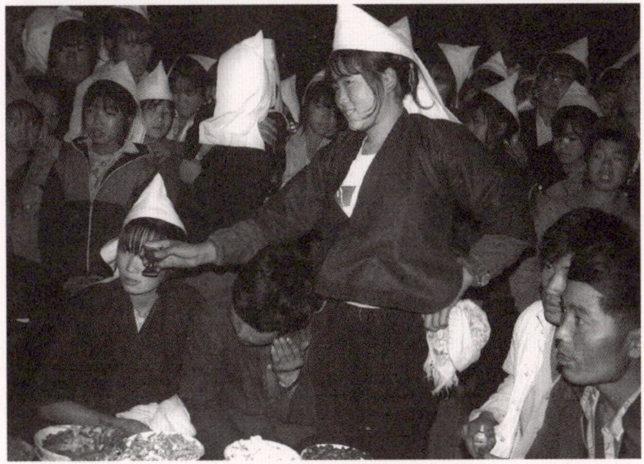

Top: Hani Yiche people grow rice and farm fish. Their short-sleeved blouses and shorts are convenient for work in the watery terraces. **Honghe County, Yunnan, 2010. Photo: Liu Jianming**

Above: Young men and women from different villages assemble for dating banquets known as *abaduo*. Under the guidance of middle-aged community members, they socialise through a series of songs and toasts. **Honghe County, Yunnan, 1993**

Right: Hani Yiche women strengthen relationships with their *cheai* (lovers) through playing musical instruments. **Honghe County, Yunnan, 1993**

Country of Daughters

—

There are around 53,000 Mosuo people living in Yunnan and Sichuan provinces. Yunnan recognises them as an ethnic group in their own right, but they are not included on the national list. In Sichuan, the Mosuo are considered part of the Mongolian ethnic group.

Top and above: A Mosuo female elder adorns a girl standing beside the designated 'female pillar' during her coming-of-age ceremony. **Ninglang County, Yunnan, 1993/2002**

It's the duty of an uncle to preside over his nephew's coming-of-age ceremony in front of the designated 'male pillar'. **Ninglang County, Yunnan, 1993/2002**

When Mosuo children reach thirteen, they undergo a clothing-change ceremony to signify coming of age. Young women put on a skirt, while young men don trousers – clothes that symbolise the gendered adult roles they will play in their community.

The ritual has special significance for young women, who will one day serve as heads of their households. Mosuo society is known for being matrilineal: Mosuo children are raised by their mother's side of the family and carry on her family name.

The Mosuo girl's coming-of-age ceremony is held next to a designated pillar inside the maternal grandmother's home and is presided over by either the girl's mother or maternal grandmother. After offering thanks to the gods and ancestors, the girl stands with one foot on a slab of pig's fat and the other on a sack of grain, which together represent the blessings of plenty. In her right hand, she holds a bracelet, beads, earrings and other adornments, symbolising beauty, and in her left she holds pieces of cotton fabric and sackcloth, symbolising talent and practical ability.

The presiding matriarch then removes the girl's childhood clothing, replacing it with a collared blouse, a pleated dress and a headscarf – the clothes of an adult Mosuo woman. A large embroidered belt is also placed around her waist, straightening her posture to give her a more adult bearing.

When the clothing change is complete, a priest joins the ceremony and prays for the young woman while placing a sheepskin cord around her neck as an auspicious ornament. The girl who is coming of age calls a dog inside and feeds it a ball of rice and a morsel of pork fat, saying, 'People only live to thirteen, but dogs live to sixty. We swapped our lifespan with you and can now live much longer. For this, we give thanks,' in reference to one of the Mosuo's founding myths. Relatives then gather to congratulate the young woman at a sumptuous feast, bringing her gifts of velvet and other luxurious fabrics, weaving tools and beautifying clothing and adornments.

Now that she has completed the change of dress, her mother will prepare a 'flower room' (the term for a woman's private bedroom) on the upper floor of the family home. This signifies that the she is ready to receive men in another of the Mosuo's unique customs, known as 'walking marriage': a woman who has come of age can receive male partners at night, who walk to her family home and leave by sunrise. If she conceives, the father may hold a celebration on the baby's one-month birthday, but the children are considered to carry on their mother's line.

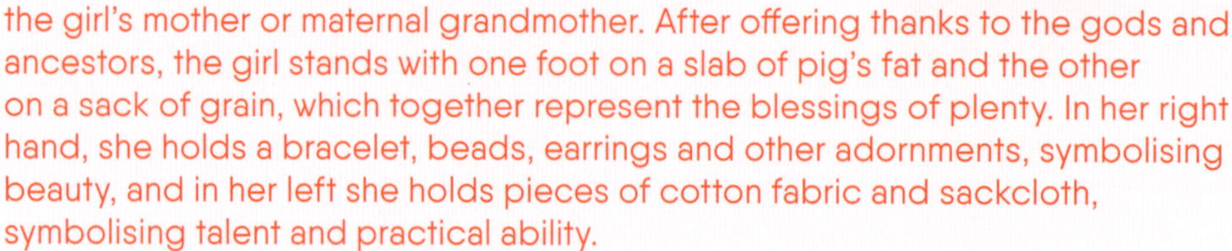

A mother dresses her daughter in the 'flower room', where Mosuo women receive lovers. **Ninglang County, Yunnan, 1995**

The Years of the Dog

At the beginning of time, when nothing died nor was born, humans and animals lived together in harmony, with no concept of life and death. But, with no limit to their lives, the world became full of bored old people and tired old animals.

The Mosuo god thought that this was wrong, believing that if the heavens aged, so too should the humans and animals. Therefore, on the eve of the lunar new year, he decided to assign a lifespan to everything under the heavens, decreeing that when the year changed, everything would age by one year.

'When I call out a lifespan,' he said, 'whoever claims it will live to that age.'

As it was the middle of the night, the Mosuo's ancestor was fast asleep. So, when the god called out '1000 years', he slept on. A night-flying swan went by, however, crying, 'Ah! Oh!', and so 1000 years of life were bestowed upon the swan.

Next, the god called out '100 years', but *still* the Mosuo's ancestor did not wake. A passing yellow duck called out in his place, and so the yellow duck would live for 100 years.

When the god called out 'sixty years', still their ancestor did not wake, and only a dog's barking could be heard. On and on it went, until the god cried out 'thirteen years', and the still-sleeping ancestor let out a snort. He had won almost no life at all.

By the time he eventually awoke, the calling was already finished, the lifespans all accounted for. Regretful and indignant, the Mosuo ancestor felt that thirteen years was too short a life and went to challenge the god. But there was simply nothing to be done, as all the allotted lifetimes were already taken. If he wanted a longer lifespan, he was told, he could only try to find an animal willing to trade.

The man went to see many animals, but none were willing to swap. All, that is, except the dog, who felt sorry for him and agreed to trade lifetimes. Ever since, humans have lived to be sixty years old, while dogs only live to thirteen.

This heavenly decree still holds sway, it is said, and so every time the year changes, the Mosuo must stay awake to ring in the new year. When Mosuo people reach the age of thirteen, the life bestowed on them by the gods is over, and they begin instead to live the life of the dog – and that is why the Mosuo coming-of-age ceremony is held at the age of thirteen.

After the coming-of-age ceremony, young Mosuo men and women dance together.
Ninglang County, Yunnan, 2002

Coming of Age

A Head Full of Love Letters

—

There are numerous branches of the Hani, including the Aini and Yiche.

For the Hani Aini people in southern Yunnan Province, the most romantic gifts come from the mountains. If a young man is interested in a young woman, he will head out into the wilderness on a winter's night, in pursuit of a rare insect – the *jinguizi*, or scarab beetle. In some communities, gathering six of these glittering green beetles for your beloved is considered the best way of expressing your true feelings, while also proving yourself brave and dedicated. If he is lucky enough to catch six scarab beetles, the young man attaches them to an artificial flower made from red beans – creating a dazzling decoration of red and green – and then sends this ornament, along with accessories such as copper bracelets, to the young woman concerned.

The scarab beetle's never-fading emerald-green shell symbolises enduring love, while red beans, with their tough shell and bright colour, symbolise loyalty. As for the copper bracelets, the fact they never rust represents a love that will not be diminished by the passage of time. If the woman is willing to consider the man as a potential lover, she will string the beetles and beans he has given her into her headdress. If he cannot find any scarab beetles, he is permitted to substitute them with a delicately carved and polished bone ornament, bearing traditional patterns and six bone needles.

I once came across a young Hani Aini woman who wore the most extravagant headdress. Gasping in admiration, I exclaimed, 'How beautiful!' – to which a nearby group of locals replied, 'Join the queue!' Seeing my bewilderment, they burst into laughter and explained that all the ornaments in an Aini woman's headdress are gifts from her suitors, so you can tell at a glance how many young men are vying for her affections. When a young woman's headdress is full of these traditional love letters, she will take time to pick one suitor to pursue a serious relationship with.

One side of the headgear of young Hani Aini women is covered with intricately carved bone needles. The other side is decorated with *jinguizi*, or scarab beetles, which are roughly the size and shape of a cicada, with a glossy, jade-like dark-green shell that glitters in the dark. This rare insect appears only on winter nights, revealed by its brilliance. Both the needles and the beetles indicate that the women have many suitors. **Xishuangbanna, Yunnan. Photo: Li Guiyun**

Top and middle: Hani Aini young women, fully adorned. Xishuangbanna, Yunnan. Photo: Li Guiyun

Bottom: Hani Aini young woman's headwear. Xishuangbanna, Yunnan, 2002

Top to bottom left: Hani Aini young women's headwear and clothing. Xishuangbanna, Yunnan, 2010
Bottom right: Hani Aini young women, fully adorned. Xishuangbanna, Yunnan, 2011. Photo: Li Jianfeng

Top: Many of the accessories worn by Hani Aini young women come from suitors – the more accessories they wear, the more suitors they have. Xishuangbanna, Yunnan, 2010. Photo: Li Jianfeng

Middle, left to right: Hani Aini youths perform the traditional bamboo dance. Pu'er, Yunnan, 2010. Photo: Tan Chun; Hani Aini young woman's headwear. Pu'er, Yunnan, 2011. Photo: Yang Wei

Bottom: Hani Aini young woman's headwear. Xishuangbanna, Yunnan, 2009. Photo: Wang Wengui

Blooming Flower

At age sixteen, Yi girls trade in their trousers or simple *shala* skirt of childhood for a rainbow-striped skirt called a *majiao*, typically made from linen.

I once witnessed this ceremonial clothing change in a Yi village near the border of Yunnan and Sichuan, presided over by a respected female elder who had been blessed with many children and grandchildren.

The ceremony was held in the room to the left of the family's firepit, as the Yi consider the left side auspicious. After worshipping the gods and spirits, the presiding elder draped a red and black woollen skirt first around the girl's head and then her thighs – red for prosperity, black for honour and dignity. The skirt represented both a blessing and the lifting of the ban prohibiting her from having sex. Friends and relatives then replaced the girl's childhood skirt with the vibrantly coloured new one, adding accessories too.

Finally, the elder held up a wooden board laden with pork and liquor, spinning it over the top of the girl's head while chanting these auspicious words:

Girl like a flower,
You have now bloomed.
You can marry and have someone to call your own.
You no longer belong to your parents;
You belong to that person of your own.
The flower blooms and bears fruit;
The girl changes dress and can now wed.

Coming-of-age clothes-changing ceremony of the Yi people in Sichuan and Yunnan. **Ninglang County, Yunnan, 1993**

The Secret Language of the Rooster Hat

Young women of the Yi and Hani ethnic groups often wear a hat resembling a rooster's comb when they come of age, as the rooster is associated with safety and happiness. Yi legend has it that long ago, there was a couple living happily together until a devil destroyed their village. The couple tried to fight the devil but struggled. At a critical moment in their tussle, the sun rose and a rooster crowed, which scared the devil away and allowed the couple to escape. The cockscomb hat honours the rooster and symbolises luck and protection.

On one visit to a Yi village in Yunnan, I watched as a young girl tried to steal the hat of an older girl to play with, upon which she was immediately admonished by an elder. Asked why, the elder explained, 'That hat signifies that she is marriageable and can bear children, and a little devil's head hasn't grown enough to create chaos!' It turns out that a girl is only permitted to wear this kind of hat once she comes of age; otherwise she will be unlucky for the rest of her life.

In some areas, however, all unmarried Yi women wear a rooster hat, no matter their age. With its evil-averting silverware and auspicious embroidery, this hat carries blessings and can improve a girl's prospects in life. According to Yi legend, it is even thought that the *yang* energy of the rooster can help its wearer to resist demons in the dark forest.

A rooster hat can be used to send different messages, depending on how it is placed. Young girls wear it straight, while women who are in a relationship wear it askew. If a young woman has found her true love, she will wear the hat backwards, as a means of warning off further suitors. After marriage, a woman is forbidden to wear the hat, as it would indicate that she is still hoping to attract suitors.

The style of the cockscomb hat worn by Yi and Hani young women reveals much about her courtship status. For Yi women living around Dianchi Lake in Yunnan, the same cockscomb hat can convey different messages depending on how it is placed on the head. **Honghe, Yunnan, 1992/1994**

Crowning a Flower Fairy

A Yi *bimo* (priest) pins a rhododendron onto the chosen girl. **Chuxiong, Yunnan. Photo: Zhang Shaoming**

Natural materials drawn from China's varied climates and topography play a key role in the colourful courtship attire of many ethnic groups. It is common for both young men and women to decorate themselves to display their beauty and talents to suitors, drawing inspiration from the natural world and changing seasons. In particular, floral adornments inspired by romantic legends bring spring courtship to life.

In the spring of 1990, I went on a trip to Yunnan to attend the Chahua Jie, or Flower Arrangement Festival, which takes place on the eighth day of the second lunar month. This Yi festival is also an occasion to celebrate young love, with couples adorning each other with flowers to express their feelings.

The rhododendron is deemed the most auspicious flower of the festival. Not only do people wear them, but they also attach bunches of these blooms to their cattle and sheep, and place them in arrangements above the entrance to the family home. There are various folk legends regarding the origin of the festival, all relating to the rhododendron. According to one legend, when great floods drowned the people of the world, only a brother and sister were left. The brother married three fairies, as well as his sister, and each gave birth to nine children; from these thirty-six children the ethnic groups of the world were repopulated. After the brother died and went to heaven, he began to miss his offspring on earth, so he descended once again into the human world. There, he turned into a large rhododendron tree in full bloom, and so Yi people adopted the rhododendron tree as their ancestral god. Every year they gather to honour the ancestors and pray for their family, livestock and homes by decorating the villages with rhododendron flowers.

On the day of the festival I attended, people from the surrounding villages gathered in a clearing in a nearby wood. To start, a *bimo* (priest) presided over a ceremony to worship the rhododendron. Each of the villages then put forward their candidate to be crowned the region's annual flower fairy. All candidates had to be eloquent, elegant, well-mannered and unmarried young women – the winner would be much sought-after by suitors. The women were decorated from head to toe with red rhododendrons, and when they walked, it was like a river of flowers flowing past.

The presiding *bimo* paced up and down in front of the candidates, ringing a bell and singing the ancient *meige* scripture of the Yi that tells of the origins of heaven, earth and humankind. When the song turned to the subject of women, the *bimo* stopped, and the candidate directly in front of him was crowned that year's flower fairy. Amid cheers from onlookers, the *bimo* arranged several bright-red rhododendrons in the flower fairy's hair.

Coming of Age

Legend has it that in ancient times, there was a young Yi shepherd woman who couldn't participate in the annual Saizhuang Festival, a celebration of traditional dress, because she had no new clothes to wear. Undeterred, she wove flowers and plants into her tattered blouse, which she adorned with the feathers of a golden pheasant that her lover, a hunter, had sent her. The young woman and her feathered, flowered costume won first place at the fashion competition that year. She later became a golden pheasant and flew away, but her skill in turning natural materials into beautiful accessories, and the embroidery techniques she shared, were passed down through the generations. She was hailed as a goddess of embroidery, and every year on the twenty-eighth day of the third lunar month, people gather to build altars in her honour. Young women from all the surrounding villages attend and exhibit their embroidery at the Saizhuang Festival, and the occasion provides an opportunity to socialise with potential suitors among the young men who come to dance, sing and find a partner.

Young Yi women participating in the Saizhuang Festival.
Chuxiong, Yunnan, 2011

The Songs of Star-Crossed Lovers

In October 1993, I travelled to the mountains near Lijiang, in north-western Yunnan, to study the folklore of the Naxi. I met a sixty-year-old Naxi woman during my time there, and when she learned of my interest in Naxi love songs, she took me to a hilltop that is considered a sacred spot for star-crossed lovers. She began to sing an ancient song that describes the place:

> Where red deer till the land and tigers are ridden,
> And we can eat for seven years from one scatter of seeds.
> There are no flies or mosquitoes,
> No pain and no suffering, no tears and no sorrow.
> When hungry you eat meat and when thirsty you drink milk.
> I want to go there with my beloved.

The rhythmic and captivating sound of her singing chimed with the rustling of the pine forest, drifting on the autumn wind around the Jade Dragon Snow Mountain. In a slightly mournful vibrato, the old woman counted off the times when someone from the village had died for love. The melody was so haunting, the portrait of love and loss so vivid and fresh, it is no wonder that the Naxi have been able to pass on their legends, beliefs, rituals and customs through so many generations.

A Naxi singer well-versed in songs about ill-fated love.
Lijiang, Yunnan, 1992

A beautiful spot where Naxi lovers meet.
Lijiang, Yunnan, 1992

Previous: The pointed white headdresses of young Hani Yiche women at a festival near Dayangjie Village, Honghe Hani Autonomous Prefecture, Yunnan.

Opposite: Hani Yiche teenagers decked out in snail-shaped silver ornaments at a festival near Dayangjie Village, Yunnan.

Hani Yiche women's traditional attire includes a *quelang*, an indigo jacket with elbow-length sleeves. Yiche women's tops traditionally had many layers to indicate wealth; modern versions are pleated for a similar effect.

The Duoyishu rice terraces at sunset in Yuanyang County, Honghe Hani and Yi Autonomous Prefecture, Yunnan. The tight-fitting shorts, or *laba*, of Hani Yiche women allowed them to easily tend the terraces for generations. Nowadays, traditional clothing is worn only at festivals.

Opposite: Young Hani Yiche women in traditional dress at a festival near Dayangjie Village, Yunnan. The back of their white headdresses is decorated with colourful embroidery.

Following: Hani Yiche teenage boys dressed up in the hope of catching a young woman's eye at a festival near Dayangjie Village, Yunnan.

Hani Yiche teenage boys
at a festival near Dayangjie
Village, Yunnan.

Opposite and following three spreads:
In preparation for a festival, a young Longhorn
Miao woman dons an elaborate headpiece
comprising a mix of wool and 'ancestral
hair', some of which has been passed
down through generations. The strands are
wrapped in a figure eight around a horn
and secured with a white ribbon. Yizhongdi
Village, Zhijin County, Guizhou.

Young Basha Miao men and women in indigo clothing. The women wear colourful aprons, and the men wear their hair in a topknot with the rest shaved.

Young Basha Miao women's
traditional dress.

Previous: Rice terraces tended by Miao people from Basha Village, Qiandongnan Miao and Dong Autonomous Prefecture, Guizhou Province.

Opposite: The headdresses of young Hani Aini women are decorated on one side with iridescent green beetles, and on the other with carved bone needles. These ornaments are gifted by suitors and indicate a young woman's popularity. Mangjia Village, Xishuangbanna Dai Autonomous Prefecture, Yunnan.

Following: Traditional Hani Aini attire at a festival in Mangjia Village, Yunnan.

Previous: The Getu River framed by forested mountains in Getu River National Park, Ziyun Miao and Buyei Autonomous County, Guizhou.

This spread: Bailuo Yi women dressed for a festival in Chengzhai Village, Wenshan Zhuang and Miao Autonomous Prefecture, Yunnan. Their clothing is woven and embroidered by hand, and often decorated with intricate batik designs.

Opposite: A young Bailuo Yi woman in festival attire, Chengzhai Village, Yunnan.

Following: Thick snow in Hongkor, Bayan Har Mountains, Qinghai.

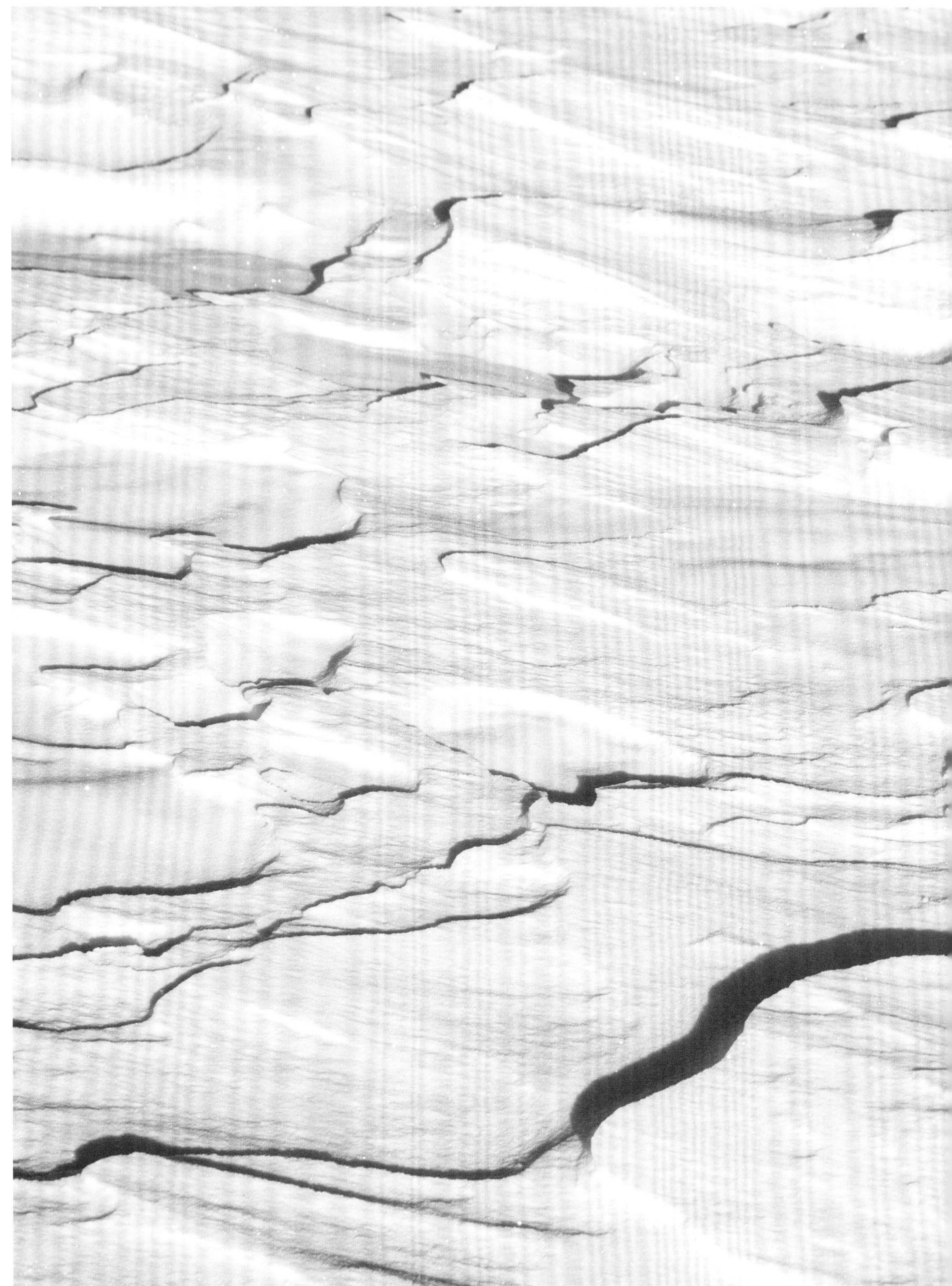

Above: Amdo Tibetan novice monks chanting prayers at a festival in Maqen County, Golog Tibetan Autonomous Prefecture, Qinghai.

Opposite: A Kham Tibetan woman dressed for winter in Hongkor.

Young Amdo Tibetan monks in
festival headdresses leading a
procession during Tibetan new year
celebrations at a temple in Maqen
County, Qinghai.

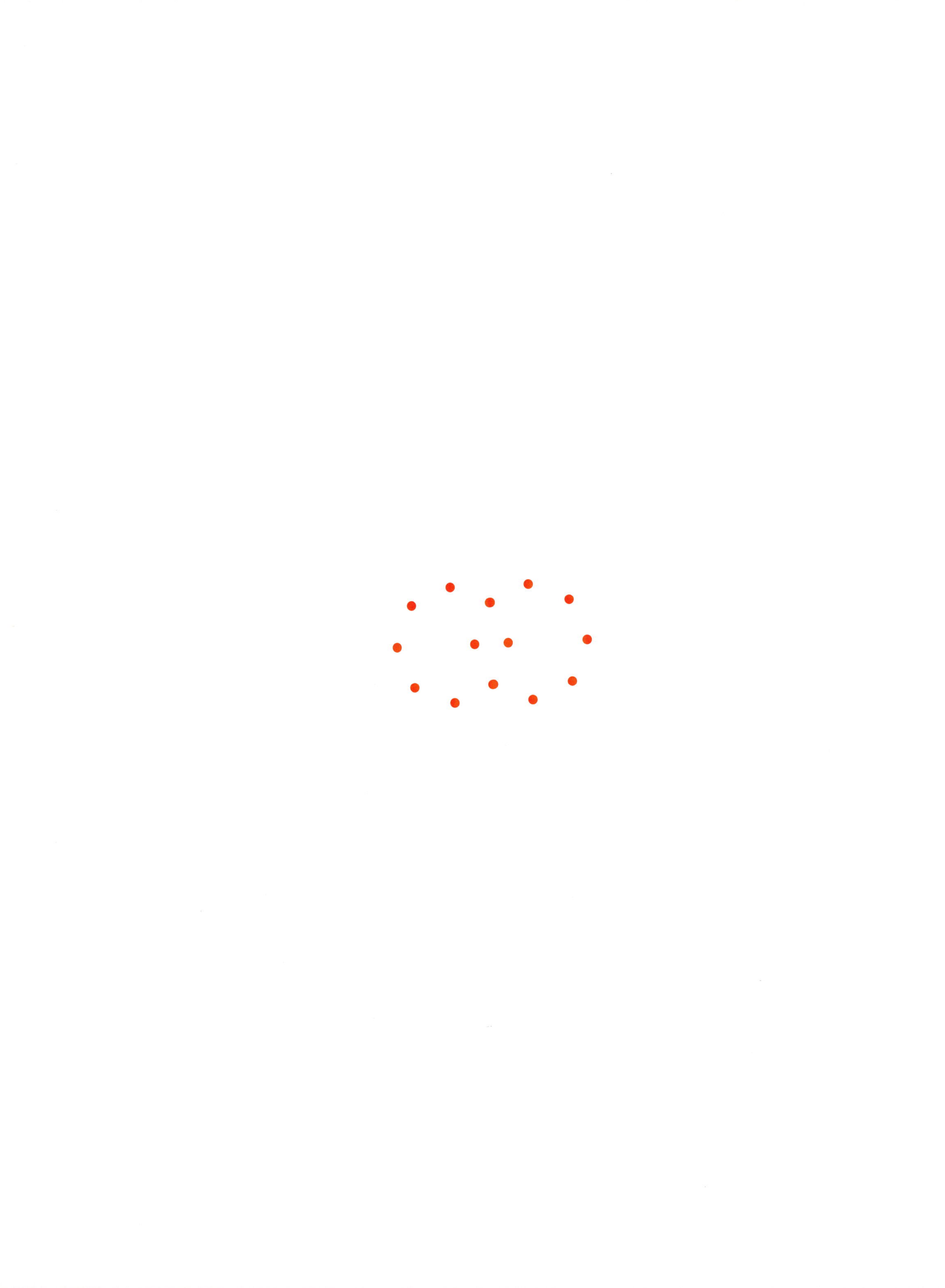

Marriage

Celebrations

03

Top: A Pan Yao bride and groom cover their faces with a fan and headscarf. Jinxiu County, Guangxi, 2009. Photo: Liang Hanchang

Bottom: Fully adorned Zhuang bride. Nandan County, Guangxi, 2008. Photo: Liang Hanchang; Tibetan women's formal adornments worn for weddings and other special occasions. Sichuan, 1995

Marriage Celebrations

It was only when I began to write this book that I realised my wife and I don't have a single photo of our wedding day. My parents' wedding picture, from the 1930s, shows my father in a Western-style suit and my mother in a white wedding dress; my father's home province of Guangdong was full of people who had gone abroad in search of work and brought such fashions back with them. But by the time my wife and I married in 1983, seven years after the end of the Cultural Revolution, borrowed Western trends and ancient Han wedding rituals alike had been lost.

In some ways, it was fortunate that no lavish attire or festivities were expected. Having enrolled at university the year after the national college entrance exam resumed in the wake of the Cultural Revolution, I was a recent graduate – and was making ¥56 (around US$9) a month. There was no wedding ring, veil, dowry or dress. I wore the bell-bottomed trousers that were popular at the time, and my wife wore a festive red blouse in a style not seen in China for many years – an emblem of the dawning of a new era.

At their heart, wedding adornments and the rituals and language that surround them signify a commitment to the all-important idea of family. A marriage heralds the possibility of children to continue the bloodline and carry on the community's culture, and wedding adornments communicate this hope for the next generation.

Of course, language is not limited to verbal and written forms. Objects, both natural and manufactured, can become part of a symbolic language in any culture, allowing for an exchange with ancestral spirits, contemporaries and the future. Weddings offer a veritable feast of such symbolism. In the course of my research, I have seen brides decked out in everything under the sun: from the ornate mirrors and feathery phoenix headdresses of the Bai, to the gold and silver of ethnic Tibetan nomads. Brides of many ethnic groups wear family-made wedding dresses decorated with a variety of meaningful patterns: clouds to symbolise matrimonial harmony, pomegranates and their flowers for fertility, or a pod of lotus seeds to promote the birth of multiple sons.

Much of the symbolism seen in wedding adornment is drawn from legend and mythology. For example, De'ang brides wear ornate rattan rings around their waists, supposedly to prevent them from flying away from their grooms, as foreshadowed by one of their creation myths. The Jingpo, on the other hand, believe that they are the descendants of the son of the Sun God and the daughter of the Water Dragon, and so must perform ceremonies to eliminate the foul smell of their female ancestor's watery scales. In every culture, the clothing and accessories worn, particularly by brides, offer insights into the cultural inheritance and prevailing attitudes towards marriage and family.

Tibetan women's formal adornments worn for weddings and other special occasions.
Sichuan, 1995

Bound Together

—

Many ethnic groups use wedding adornments to represent the bond between bride and groom. The rattan rings of the De'ang, the silver chains of the Miao and the hooped headdresses of the Mongolians all signify that the husband is drawing on the power of the gods to cement his relationship with his wife.

In China's south-west, home to many ethnic minority groups, folk celebrations often take place in early spring. The subtropical climate makes for warm winters and hot, humid summers. February, a mild, sunny and relatively dry month, marks a time of house building, marriage and festivals.

In February 1993, I visited the De'ang township of Santaishan, on the outskirts of the city of Mangshi in Yunnan Province, with some filmmaker friends. We were there to make an ethnographic documentary and, as luck would have it, we stumbled across a wedding in a nearby De'ang village. The villagers, magnificently dressed and in high spirits, sat outside a bamboo house around wicker tables drinking liquor. The hospitable host spotted us, guests from afar, and eagerly invited us to join them.

A well-dressed community elder was sitting in the main room, exchanging blessings with the bridegroom. Melancholic farewell songs filled the air, as they would have done for the last three days and nights, setting a solemn tone for the ceremonies to come. Some spoke of the anguish of a mother being separated from her daughter, who would go to live with her husband's family; others spoke of their grief for a soon-to-depart friend. (Only later did I find out that those singing farewell songs to the bride included her former suitors.) The bride's mother sat next to the bride shedding silent tears, while the bride cried inconsolably.

Eventually, the seemingly endless stream of tears came to an abrupt halt, and we accompanied the bride as she set out on the road to the groom's family home. When she arrived, her bridesmaids helped her into the new dress and accessories given to her by her mother-in-law. The bride replaced her coloured headscarf with a black turban – indicating to other men that she was now unavailable – and put on earrings and a series of neckbands and bracelets. Over her straight skirt, she wore another skirt gifted by her in-laws, signifying that she had joined her husband's family. Finally, she lifted a large pile of rattan hoops and fastened them around her waist.

Rattan hoops – a special feature of De'ang women's adornments and an integral part of De'ang weddings – have mythical origins. The De'ang believe that humankind was born out of a gourd; the men who emerged all looked alike, and it was impossible to tell one from another. As for the women, as soon as they appeared, they flew into the sky, not wanting to stay with the men below. The gods later used their powers to distinguish men's faces and helped the men to 'bind' women to them with rattan hoops worn around the waist. Thus, women could no longer fly and instead stayed and lived with the men.

Traditionally, De'ang women wear short, tight-fitting tops and long skirts, encircled at the waist by as many as thirty hoops, painted red and black. These are usually made entirely of rattan, or occasionally half rattan and half silver. The number and quality of hoops a woman wears is considered to be a measure of her status and wealth. A De'ang man will carefully craft rattan hoops engraved with auspicious patterns of flowers and birds for the woman he loves, as a demonstration of his skill and a sign of his admiration. When the couple marries, the wearing of these hoops signifies that the bride will remain true to the groom.

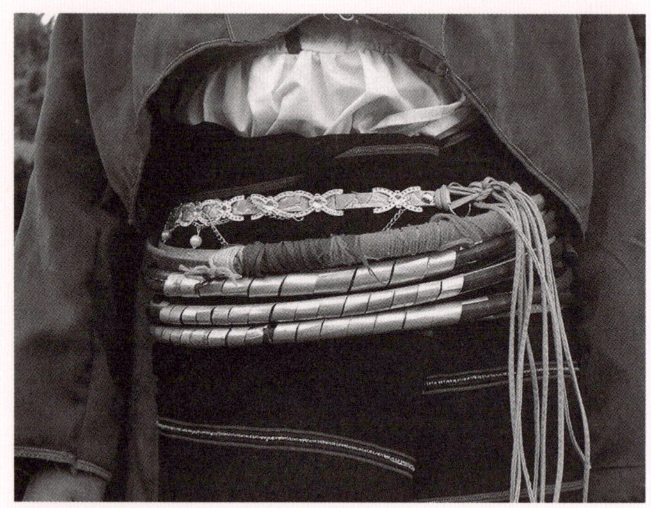

De'ang woman's waistbands. Zhenkang County, Yunnan. Photo: Liu Jianming

Marriage Celebrations

Scenes from a De'ang village. **Dehong, Yunnan, 2001/2016**

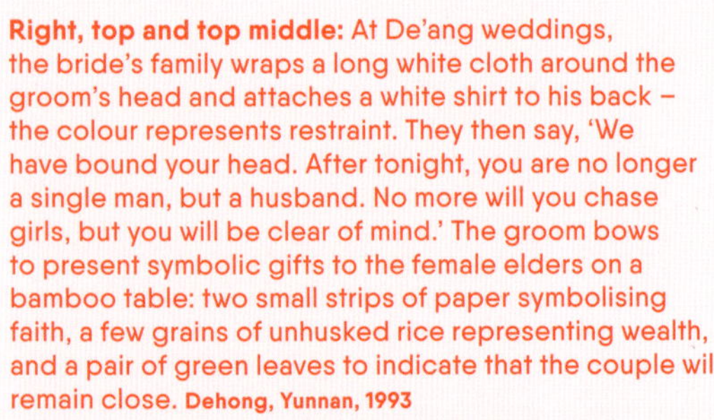

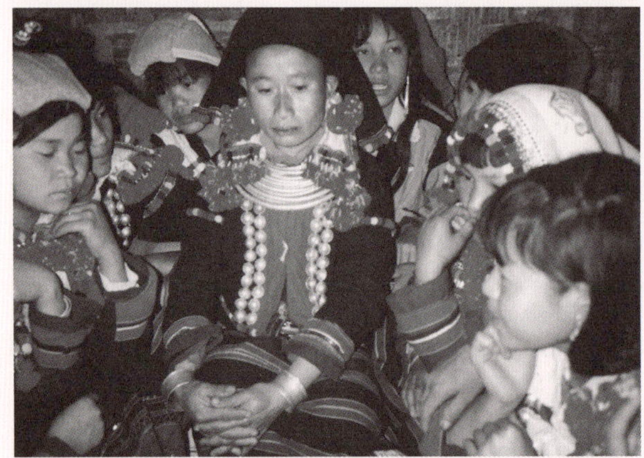

Right, top and top middle: At De'ang weddings, the bride's family wraps a long white cloth around the groom's head and attaches a white shirt to his back – the colour represents restraint. They then say, 'We have bound your head. After tonight, you are no longer a single man, but a husband. No more will you chase girls, but you will be clear of mind.' The groom bows to present symbolic gifts to the female elders on a bamboo table: two small strips of paper symbolising faith, a few grains of unhusked rice representing wealth, and a pair of green leaves to indicate that the couple will remain close. **Dehong, Yunnan, 1993**

Right, bottom middle and bottom: When the groom arrives, the bride forms a circle with her friends – crying and embracing them. Her former lovers and other young men cover their heads with a cotton blanket and sing a sad song with the young women. **Dehong, Yunnan, 1993**

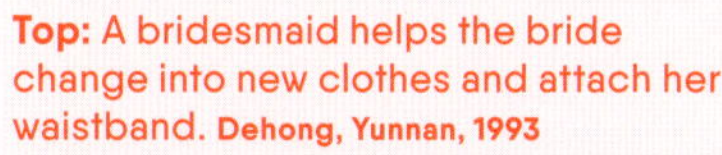

Top: A bridesmaid helps the bride change into new clothes and attach her waistband. **Dehong, Yunnan, 1993**

Middle, left and center: A bridesmaid helps the bride arrange her adornments.

Middle, right: A singer dressed up for the wedding. **Dehong, Yunnan, 1993**

Bottom: The bride wakes early on the next morning to start cooking for her in-laws, demonstrating her virtue and talent. **Santaishan Township, Mangshi City, Dehong Dai and Jingpo Autonomous Prefecture, Yunnan, 1993**

Left, top to bottom: Guoshan Yao women attending a wedding. Hezhou, Guangxi, 2010. Photo: Liang Hanchang; A Guoshan Yao bride and groom dressed for their wedding. Hezhou, Guangxi, 2010. Photo: Liang Hanchang

Right, top and middle: A Yao wedding. Hezhou, Guangxi, 2010. Photo: Liang Hanchang

Right, bottom: A Yao bride and groom dressed for their wedding. Hezhou, Guangxi, 2009. Photo: Liang Hanchang

An Auspicious Day

In the autumn of 2018, I travelled with a group to western Yunnan to visit Zhoucheng, a Bai village on the outskirts of Dali. There were quite a few weddings taking place during our trip, which coincided with auspicious dates in both the Gregorian and lunar calendars.

Bai weddings in the region are usually held over four days. We had arrived on the third day of one such marriage celebration, just in time for the main event, called *zhengxi*. A coloured marquee stood by the entrance to the courtyard home, and the guests were so numerous that the kitchen could barely cope. We battled through the great clouds of steam that were billowing from the huge cooking pots and saw that the feast spilled out across the courtyard and into the main hall.

A middle-aged woman wearing Bai traditional dress gave us permission to join in the celebration, and we repaid the family's hospitality with a *hongbao* – a red envelope of lucky money that is the customary gift at Chinese weddings.

After the feast, the groom and several family elders made offerings to the ancestors and spirits. With the host's permission, we went upstairs to find the bride. She was wearing a long pink dress, seated on a wooden stool in a small room bursting with her friends. Her feet were resting on a wooden bucket full of millet with an oil lamp placed on top – symbolising a future married life of plenty and bright prospects. A middle-aged woman combed her hair and helped her put on betrothal gifts from the groom's family: necklaces, rings, earrings, bracelets and other adornments made of gold, silver and jade. Of these, it is the jade bracelet and silver 'eel-bone' ornaments that are essential to show her status as a married woman – from the day of her wedding onwards, a woman must wear a jade bracelet on her left wrist and a chain in the shape of an eel bone attached to the right side of her jacket.

Suddenly the air was filled with the shrill sound of the *suona*, a traditional wind instrument. A bridesmaid explained that the bride's parents and family elders were about to hold a ceremony to receive the groom. We went downstairs as the bride's father adorned the groom's chest with a flower pin for happiness and joy, and hung red decorations – a celebratory colour – around him. The groom then made a toast before going upstairs to bring the bride down.

We watched as a family elder handed the bride a sewing needle and thimble, which represent quarrelling. Led by a female elder, the bridal party headed out, carrying the betrothal gifts. When the group reached the head of the bridge over a nearby river, the bride threw the needle and thimble into the water to indicate her wish for a smooth and untroubled marriage.

Before the Bai bride departs, an elderly relative feeds her a mouthful of food with chopsticks. **Dali, Yunnan, 2018**

Marriage Celebrations

Bride wearing bronze mirror. Dali, Yunnan, 2018

—

An essential part of any Bai wedding dress is a bronze mirror, worn like a pendant to repel wandering evil spirits, who are thought to fear their own reflections. This protection also extends to the couple's new home as, upon entering, the bride must remove the mirror from her dress and hang it facing the doorway, in order to drive away evil spirits from the house. Ancient mirrors were made from polished bronze. Nowadays, glass mirrors are increasingly common at Bai wedding ceremonies. In some areas, new brides are even given sunglasses to wear to protect their gaze from evil spirits.

Right, top to bottom: The bride rests her feet on a wooden bucket full of millet with an oil lamp placed on top, while friends help her get ready. Dali, Yunnan, 2018; At the sound of the *suona*, the groom pays his respects to his new in-laws before going upstairs to greet the bride. Dali, Yunnan, 2018; The bride and bridesmaids. Dali, Yunnan, 2018; The family takes a group photo before the bride and groom depart. Dali, Yunnan, 2018. All photos this page: Cat Vinton

A Royal Region

—

Feng shui literally translates as 'wind and water', and the term refers to a set of beliefs around the placement of objects to allow for the proper flow of qi, or life force.

—

A Bai bride will also wear an embroidered shawl and a zisun (meaning 'offspring') satchel that conveys blessings to her future children.

The phoenix is widely perceived to be an auspicious symbol in China, but the mythical bird has special significance for the Bai and features prominently in traditional wedding attire. The bride will often wear a tall ornamental wreath, decorated with a variety of pompoms, silk flowers and coloured beads, with a golden phoenix in the centre.

Folk legend has it that the feng shui is particularly good in the Bai region of Cang Mountain and Er Lake, famous scenic areas around the city of Dali in Yunnan. There is also a strong sense of royalty in the nearby Phoenix Mountain, as the region was home to the kings of the ancient kingdoms of Dali and Nanzhao. After the Tang (618–907) and Song (960–1279) dynasties, the central court even dispatched men to destroy its powerful feng shui, so worried were they about this area claiming independence. To commemorate the glorious history the Phoenix Mountain had bestowed on them, local people created the phoenix-crown headdress.

Above and bottom: The Bai ethnic group predominantly live in the foothills of Cang Mountain and on the banks of Er Lake.

Phoenix headdress. **Dali, Yunnan, 2018. Photo: Cat Vinton**

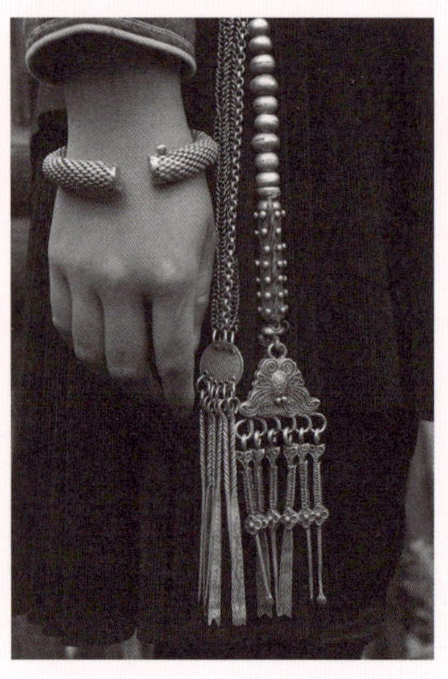

Top and middle left: Zhuang silver jewellery. Napo County, Guangxi. Photo: Liang Hanchang

Middle right to bottom, left to right: Black-Clothes Zhuang outfit. Napo County, Guangxi. Photo: Liang Hanchang; Zhuang silver jewellery. Congjiang County, Guizhou, 2008. Photo: Liang Hanchang; Black-Sand Zhuang clothing and accessories. Qubei County, Yunnan, 2008. Photo: Liang Hanchang

Top and middle, left to right: Zhuang bridal outfit. Longsheng County, Guangxi, 2008. Photo: Liang Hanchang; Zhuang silver jewellery. Napo County, Guangxi. Photo: Liang Hanchang; Jin Nong Zhuang women. Wenshan, Yunnan, 2008. Photo: Liang Hanchang; Black–Sand Zhuang headdress. Qiubei County, Yunnan, 2008. Photo: Liang Hanchang

Bottom: Fully adorned Zhuang women. Wenshan, Yunnan, 2008. Photo: Liang Hanchang

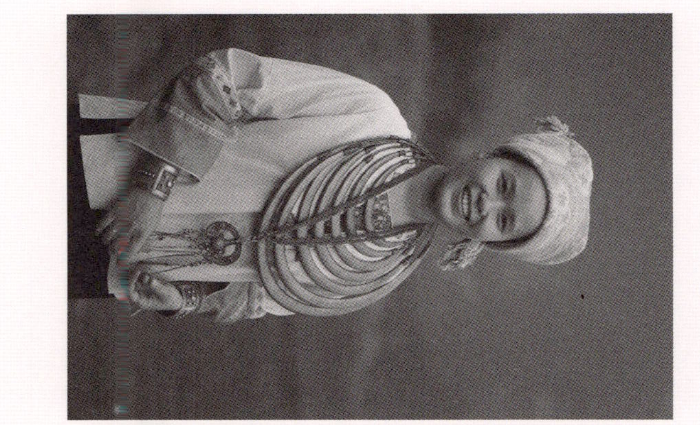

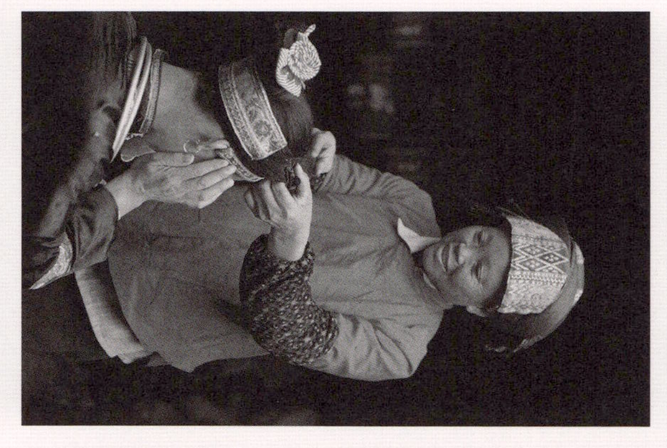

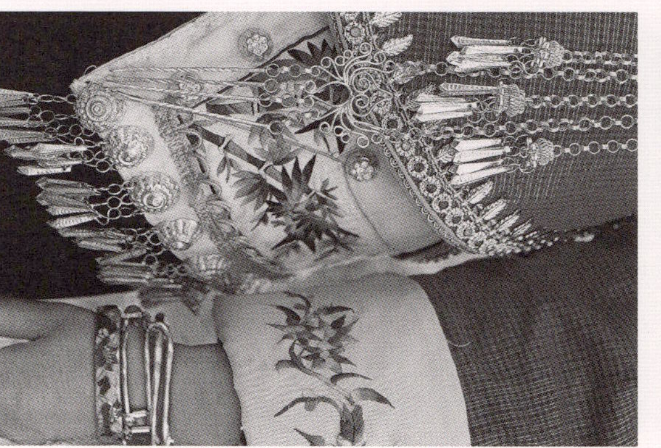

Top: At a Huatou Yao wedding, the mother of the bride dresses her daughter. Fangchenggang, Guangxi, 2007. Photo: Liang Hanchang

Middle: The bride's elder brother carries his sister. Fangchenggang, Guangxi, 2007. Photo: Liang Hanchang

Bottom, left to right: A wedding send-off from relatives. Fangchenggang, Guangxi, 2007. Photo: Liang Hanchang; Final touches before the bride enters the groom's house. Fangchenggang, Guangxi, 2007. Photo: Liang Hanchang

Yao bridesmaids and groomsmen in traditional dress. **Jiangcheng, Yunnan, 2009**

Wearable Treasures

Since I first visited Diqing Tibetan Autonomous Prefecture in north-western Yunnan in 1977, I have returned time and again, enchanted not only by the region's historical significance on an ancient tea-trading route, but also by the beautiful folk customs and the bold, uninhibited character of its people. Under the blue dome of a May sky, with wildflowers blooming across the grassy plateaus of Shangri-La, some 3000 metres above sea level, it feels close to paradise.

Ethnic Tibetan brides are among the most lavishly adorned I have encountered. Before the ceremony, the groom will send his bride a silk-wrapped bundle of beautiful clothing and jewellery for her to wear for the wedding, as well as tassels adorned with mirrors and jade. When the bridal party arrives at the groom's home, he will attach these tassels to the back of the bride's dress, to show that she now belongs to his family.

As nomadic herders, Tibetans use elaborate adornment as a way of carrying their valuables on their person as they move from place to place. During any special celebration, it's common to see Tibetan women draped from head to toe with treasures rich in monetary and cultural value: gold, silver, pearls, agate, rare turquoise, beeswax balls and dzi beads, as well as invaluable scrolls, ancient Buddha statues and other artefacts.

One Tibetan man I encountered on a trip to the region explained the custom: 'We Tibetans aren't like you. We don't have fixed abodes in which we can store our valuables. The tent is our movable home, and the yak and sheep our property. Every year we sell off a few yak or sheep in order to get by, and to buy jewels for our women. Wearing such jewels, our women are beautiful and precious; they are the guardians of Tibetan men's resources, in respect of both love and wealth.'

The Tibetan Plateau, 1999

Right: The high pastures of the Tibetan Plateau, 1999

Bottom: The Tibetan Xuan dance.
Kejia Temple, Tibet, 2016. Photo: Ren Yunjuan

Marriage Celebrations

Tibetan women's adornments. Tibet, Yunnan and Sichuan, 1995

Marriage Celebrations

Top: Tibetan women's attire. Ngari, Tibet, 2014. Photo: Ren Yunjuan

Bottom: Tibetan women's adornments. Tibet, Yunnan and Sichuan, 1995

212

Tibetan women's adornments from Tibet and Sichuan. Qinghai Tibetan
Culture Museum, Xining, Qinghai

Marriage Celebrations

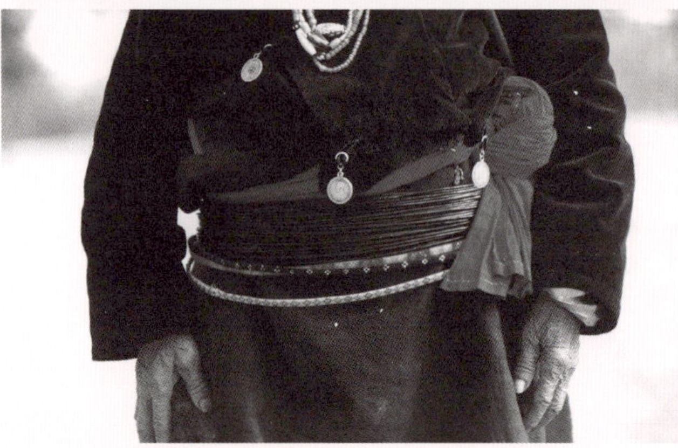

Above: Jingpo woman's waist accessories. Dehong, Yunnan, 2009. Photo: Liu Jianming

—

*Jingpo people, both men
and women, like to adorn
themselves with brightly
coloured pompoms – in red
for happiness, yellow for love
and white for purity. Similar
decorations are worn by the
De'ang and Lahu.*

—

*Jingpo bridal outfits vary, but
they may include a collarless
black top and shawl decorated
with silver baubles, and a richly
embroidered straight red skirt.*

Below: Jingpo woman in full
traditional dress. Dehong, Yunnan, 1993

Feathers of the Sun God, Scales of the Water Dragon

The Jingpo believe their oldest human ancestor was descended from the Sun God. This ancestor – a man of the sky known for adorning himself in feathers – married the Water Dragon's daughter, whose scales then turned into silver baubles. Yet this union of sky and sea was not a match made in heaven: the bride found she could not get pregnant owing to the lingering smell from her water-dwelling past. Instructed by a spirit, the groom gathered thatch, shaped like daggers, and built a grass bridge for his bride to pass over to remove the odour. Later, she did indeed become pregnant.

The grass bridge has become an important ritual at Jingpo weddings. On the day of the wedding, the groom's family gathers bunches of fragrant lemongrass to lay in front of the main entrance to their and the groom's house. When the bride is received at this house, soon to be her new home, she toasts her relatives and the village elders in front of the grass bridge. Meanwhile, a local priest communicates with the spirits and sacrifices an animal, splashing the blood onto the grass. With a basket on her back containing the dowry – a crucial element of which is *jianpa*, a beautifully embroidered satchel she will give to her husband – the bride is led by her mother-in-law across the grass bridge, with her new husband following behind. Only then can the bride set foot in the family home. The Jingpo believe that not crossing the grass bridge will hinder a bride's ability to bear children.

The act of crossing a bridge has special significance in Jingpo weddings. **Dehong, Yunnan, 1993**

Previous: A Kham Tibetan woman wearing coral and turquoise jewellery in Hongkor, Bayan Har Mountains, Qinghai.

Opposite: A Kham Tibetan woman with coral and turquoise jewellery tending her herd of yaks in Hongkor, Qinghai. Yak hides provide wool and leather to make clothing, rope, tents and traditional boats, while the animals' bones can be carved into beautiful accessories.

Above: Tibetan people have named their land Kangjong, meaning 'Land of Snows', an area isolated by high mountains and vast plateaus.

Opposite: A Kham Tibetan woman collecting water in Hongkor, Qinghai.

A traditional Dai wedding dress
in Mandan Village, Dehong
Dai and Jingpo Autonomous
Prefecture, Yunnan.

Opposite: Kham Tibetans wear beautiful accessories over their finest *chuba* during Losar new year celebrations. Dege County, Garze Tibetan Autonomous Prefecture, Sichuan.

Right: Intricate hand embroidery covering River Miao festival dress, Shidong Town, Qiandongnan Miao and Dong Autonomous Prefecture, Guizhou.

Opposite and following:
Traditional wedding attire in
Mandan Village, Yunnan.

Previous: Kham Tibetan boys wearing festival attire in Dege County, Sichuan.

Opposite: A Tibetan temple on the morning of Losar, a new year celebration. Juniper burns, filling the cold air at sunrise, in Dege, Sichuan.

This spread: Intricate Amdo Tibetan woman's adornments at a festival in Maqen County, Qinghai.

This and following spread:
Relatives help dress a Bai bride,
whose feet rest on a wooden box
containing grain and an oil lamp –
symbols of a prosperous marriage.
Zhoucheng Village, Dali Bai
Autonomous Prefecture, Yunnan.

A Bai bride wearing a bronze mirror
to repel wandering evil spirits in
Zhoucheng Village, Dali, Yunnan.

Opposite and following spread:
Four-Seal Miao festival attire is
made from hemp fabric woven
on a loom and embellished with
embroidery and batik designs,
including a pattern of four square
seal shapes. Silver jewellery and
a long rope of 'ancestral hair'
worn as a headpiece complete
the outfit. Qiaoliang Village,
Liuzhi County, Guizhou.

A Kham Tibetan woman wearing
coral and turquoise accessories at
a festival in Dege County, Sichuan.

A Kham Tibetan woman with coral and turquoise jewellery tending her herd of yaks in Hongkor, Qinghai.

Previous: Sunrise over a remote
Miao Baibei Village, high in the
Mountain Moon region, near
Rongjiang, Guizhou.

Opposite: A Kham Tibetan woman
with coral and turquoise accessories
attending Losar new year
celebrations at Dzongsar Monastery
in Dege County, Sichuan.

Silver adornments of the River Miao
in Shidong Town, Guizhou.

This spread: The River Miao village of Shidong, located in Shidong Town, Guizhou, is known for handcrafted silverware. Shidong silversmiths travel to nearby villages before festivals to replace the worn silver ornaments on festival attire. Following the celebrations, the silver pieces are then unstitched and stored separately to prevent blackening.

Amdo Tibetan festival dress in
Maqen County, Qinghai.

A Kham Tibetan woman
with coral and turquoise
accessories attending Losar
new year celebrations at
Dzongsar Monastery in Dege
County, Sichuan.

A Kham Tibetan woman with coral
and turquoise accessories attending
Losar new year celebrations in Dege
County, Sichuan.

Falling Leaves Return to Their Roots

04

Top and right: Most older people wish to be surrounded by their children and grandchildren, and older Kazakh women are no different. *Yili, Xinjiang, 2014*

Left: A fully adorned older Kazakh woman, whose whip – a symbol of honour for elders – does not leave her hand. *Yili, Xinjiang, 2014*

Falling Leaves Return to Their Roots

Good fortune as boundless as the East China Sea,
Longevity as great as the South Mountain;
Good health to all your family,
Four generations under one roof.
— Birthday blessings for a family elder

It is said that newly made gambiered Canton gauze clothing used to be uncomfortable initially, owing to its coarse fibres, and would only soften after a period of wear, so wealthy people would first give their new silk garments to their servants to wear in. Nowadays, production techniques have improved, and people can wear such clothing without discomfort.

Elders are not only the nucleus of a Chinese family, but also that of the broader community. They serve as the link between the ancestors and their living descendants, as intermediaries between the mortal and spirit worlds. Therefore, respect for the elderly and filial piety are core values in traditional Chinese society.

Many ethnic groups have special festivals and attire to honour those whose status has been elevated to communing with the ancestors. The most senior members of a family or community often become respected high priests – the imparters and inheritors of traditional culture – or even the enforcers of the law. When one enters the homes of some ethnic groups, it is immediately apparent from their adornments that elders are held in high esteem and command universal respect.

The death of such a valued person is more than the passing of an individual; it is a major family event, requiring a grand burial ceremony. If the person had a particularly long life, then the funeral is very much seen as a happy occasion. It is crucial to have the appropriate funeral adornments to meet one's ancestors – archaeological studies of grave sites the world over suggest that burial articles were not only prepared for the deceased to use in the afterlife, but also as a tribute to previous ancestors.

For close to seventy years – following the Xinhai Revolution of 1911 – faith, tradition, culture and folklore were denounced and banished in China. Many families were devastated by political upheaval; the living barely knew how to get by, while the dead couldn't connect with their ancestors. Now, some forty years since the start of China's economic reforms, funeral and other folk traditions have been rekindled. People seem keen to rebuild their faith in the cultural ruins of a political earthquake, seeking the forgiveness and blessing of their ancestors.

A practice shared by many ethnic groups in China is for an elderly person to select a piece of clothing or an accessory from their hometown to wear when they pass away. This stems from the idea that if you aren't buried wearing the traditional adornments of your community, your ancestors will not recognise you. I believe it is the wish of almost all people, in their last moment of life, to return to the source.

My grandfather died before I was born, but in the one faded photograph my father has of him, he is wearing the famous silk fabric of his home province, Guangdong. My father spoke fondly of this precious fabric, which feels cool to the touch and rustles as it moves; known as 'gambiered Canton gauze', it is made from silk that has been dyed with yam extract, processed with mineral-rich mud from riverbeds and dried in the sun.

My father also spoke of my grandfather's grandfather, who, like many men of his generation, left Guangdong and went overseas to earn a living, often through hard labour or by trading in silk and porcelain. All those men, whether they made their fortune or found themselves in dire straits, had the same wish: to wear Guangdong silk in the sunset years of their lives. I believe this was also the wish of my grandfather when he went to the photography studio – still very rare in those days – to have a picture taken in his shiny Han Chinese-style silk jacket. After my grandfather died overseas, that photograph was brought back to his hometown to be presented to his children, grandchildren and future generations.

Zhuang longevity shoes.
Xichou County, Yunnan, 2008.
Photo: Liang Hanchang

Elders wearing happiness and longevity clothing and adornments:

Top: Rukai Gaoshan couple. Pingtung, Taiwan, 2013. Photo: Lin Tianfu

Bottom left: Rukai Gaoshan couple. Pingtung, Taiwan, 2013. Photo: Lin Tianfu

Bottom right: Amis Gaoshan couple. Hualien, Taiwan, 2008. Photo: Lin Tianfu

Elders wearing happiness and longevity clothing and adornments:

Top and middle, left to right: Bunong Gaoshan couple. Taiwan, 2007. Photo: Lin Tianfu; Saixia Gaoshan couple. Taiwan, 2007. Photo: Lin Tianfu; Dawu Gaoshan couple. Taitung, Taiwan, 2006. Photo: Lin Tianfu; Kavalan Gaoshan couple. Hualien, Taiwan, 2007. Photo: Lin Tianfu; Truku Gaoshan couple. Hualien, Taiwan, 2007. Photo: Lin Tianfu

Bottom: Amis Gaoshan elders wearing tree-bark clothing and accessories, part of their ethnic group's intangible cultural heritage. Taitung, Taiwan, 2006

Falling Leaves Return to Their Roots

Status Symbols

Among the Hani Aini people in the Xishuangbanna region of Yunnan Province, it is a great honour to be elevated to the status of family elder. As a man ascends the ancestral ladder, most typically when he becomes a grandfather, he no longer needs to toil to make a living. So long as no one in the family is sick or destitute – a sign that the family is not prey to evil spirits – the man becomes the object of the family's admiration and accepts a change of clothes and a headdress to mark his new position.

Newly anointed male Hani Aini elders change into blue clothing and replace the old green headdresses they've worn since their coming-of-age rites with red ones – red being the colour associated with the gods. An elderly man with a red headcloth enjoys high prestige in the village. The red headcloth and other elder adornments are known as 'longevity clothing'; wearing them while alive means that the elder's soul has been aligned with the ancestors, and his name will be included in the ancestral lineage. From that moment on, he does not have to worry about the daily round of human life and its chores. Although he has not yet left this world, his soul has been raised above the mortal plane.

Once a Hani Aini woman becomes a grandmother, her dress tends to be uniformly cyan (a colour associated with dignity), and she wears a silver-decorated headdress to show her nobility. If her family affairs are in good order, she will receive a *wuqi* longevity headdress covered in 105 silver baubles that shine in the sun, like a god's crown. The number 105 represents perfection to the Hani people, and the silver baubles are arranged in patterns indicating that all the wishes of the grandmother's life have been satisfied.

Older Hani Aini are honoured guests at special elder-worship ceremonies, where they drink the local rice wine and sing songs passed down to them from their own elders, the words of which speak mostly of clan legends. Young men sit to one side, offering assistance when necessary; young women give back massages. On a research trip in 1993, I met an old man at one of these ceremonies and he told me that community members who lived to sixty or seventy years of age were usually blessed with many children and grandchildren, sometimes even the ideal set-up of 'four generations under one roof'.

Other ethnic groups have different clothing customs to highlight the status of respected elders. Senior members of Wa communities in Yunnan replace their usual black headscarf with a red one. Yao elders in the Guangxi Zhuang Autonomous Region and Zhuang elders in Yunnan both wear embroidered shoes bearing the character for *shou* (meaning 'longevity') and other auspicious patterns. Ethnic Kazakhs in the Xinjiang Uyghur Autonomous Region have a long legacy of falconry; symbols of honour for older men include whips, belts and gauntlets for eagles to perch on, while embroidered headdresses and pendants worn on the forehead are common among older women.

The *fanbu* ritual is an ancient practice used by many ethnic groups to celebrate their elders, who receive special clothes to wear and attend a feast in their honour. The ceremony runs on a twelve-year cycle, and each age is accompanied by the appropriate blessings: sixty-one is associated with longevity, as the elder still has many years ahead; seventy-three with health, which may have grown more fragile; and eighty-five with peace, the most important thing when one reaches such an advanced age. On the day of these ceremonies, children and grandchildren will bless their elders by feeding them meatballs – this act embodies *fanbu*, or repaying the elders for nurturing them in life.

The 100-year-old Yao elder Huang Malun and her handmade longevity shoes.
Bama County, Guangxi, 2012. Photo: Zhang Yuan

Falling Leaves Return to Their Roots

Pathways to the Spirit World

Right: During the La Mugu ('pulling the wooden drum') ceremony, a Wa shaman, with his head wrapped in a red cloth headscarf, leads the people in a series of sacred rituals, and young women feed and toast their respected elders. **Ximeng County, Yunnan, 1993**

Below: Gaoshan hat adorned with animal horns and teeth. **Shung Ye Museum of Formosan Aborigines, Taipei, Taiwan, 2006**

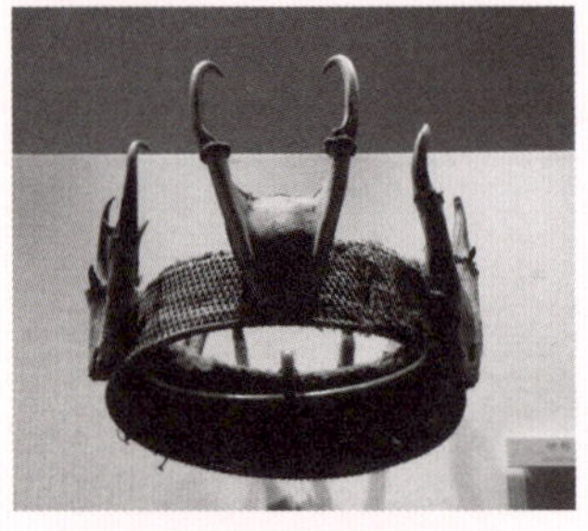

In many Chinese traditions, there is a general belief that human beings are made up of three elements: body, soul and spirit. The body is the mortal vessel, the soul allows us to communicate with fellow humans, and the spirit allows us to communicate with the gods.

The family elder with the highest *beifen* (meaning 'seniority') is considered the closest to the ancestral spirit world. Therefore, among many ethnic groups, this elder will serve as a shaman or priest. The elders who preside over sacred ceremonies are adorned with accessories that symbolise their proximity to the spirits, and even their control over the natural landscape of mountains and rivers. These mystical accessories are thought to have the capacity to open pathways between the mortal and spirit worlds.

Ornaments with spiritual qualities are usually made of materials such as animal teeth and bones, feathers, beads, jade, gold and silver. For example, during ceremonies conducted by the Wa people, the shaman and village head hold sacred red leaves from the rambutan tree in their hands and thread them through their pierced ears, as a symbol of the power granted to them by the Sun God. The talons hanging from the *douli* headdresses of the Yi *bimo* (priests) during official ceremonies symbolise the power of the dharma – the universal truth in Buddhist and other traditions. And shamans in the Himalayan region wear snake-bone necklaces to invoke the snake gods for protection during healing rituals.

Atayal Gaoshan horned headdress. **Miaoli County, Taiwan, 2013. Photo: Lin Tianfu**

Top and middle left: Headdress and necklace of a Naxi *dongba* (priest). **Lijiang, Yunnan, 1993–2006**

Right: Standard attire and accessories for a Naxi *dongba* include: a *wushen* (five gods) headdress – representing the four cardinal directions plus the centre – a red headscarf and gown, a white sheepskin shawl, a beaded necklace, sacred texts, a rattle and a long sword. **Lijiang, Yunnan, 2006**

Top: *Dongba* (priests) are the inheritors of Naxi traditional culture. **Lijiang, Yunnan, 2006**

Middle: A *dongba* holding a rattle and a long sword presides over a ritual ceremony in a village. **Lijiang, Yunnan, 2006**

Bottom: A central aim of Naxi scholars who study *dongba* culture is to pass on knowledge of its rituals. **Lijiang, Yunnan, 2006**

Dressing to Meet the Ancestors

When it comes to the importance of the funeral, China's ethnic groups are unanimous. The last of life's great ceremonies – the last change of dress – it marks the point when, the saying goes, 'falling leaves return to their roots'.

The threshold between life and death is often considered mysterious. If everything is handled properly, the soul of the deceased will be at peace, allowing it to make the transition and enter back into the cycle of reincarnation. If not handled properly, the soul of the deceased cannot return as desired, but will become a wandering ghost who brings suffering to both the living and the dead. Though there is a wide variety of ceremonies and taboos associated with funeral rites, most reflect the respect – tinged with fear – of the unknowable underworld and the restless soul of the deceased. This idea is captured in a well-known Wa saying: 'You can negotiate with a mountain of people, but you can't talk to a dead man.'

The dressing of the dead in traditional clothing is one common custom that can help ensure a smooth journey back to the land of the ancestors. Funeral dress is imbued with spiritual significance that transcends the material value of the clothing itself – which can be anything from imperial gold and jade attire to a commoner's gown symbolising filial piety.

Gaoshan beaded clothing and accessories. It is customary to dress the deceased in traditional attire, and exquisitely made clothing is often buried with the dead.
Shung Ye Museum of Formosan Aborigines, Taipei, Taiwan, 2006

The Hundred-Bird Gown

—

The base fabric of the hundred-bird gown is a local tubu (handmade cloth). Each section uses thin slices cut from silkworm cocoons to create a white background for a multiplicity of hand-embroidery techniques and stitches.

There is a widespread belief that if you are not dressed correctly in death, the ancestors won't know who you are. For example, the hundred-bird gown may be worn by the Miao people in Guizhou Province for ceremonial celebrations, but it is also a means of facilitating recognition by the ancestors. The gown derives from the Miao creation myth, in which a maple tree gave birth to a butterfly that laid twelve eggs. These butterfly eggs were hatched by a bird, thereby creating humans and all other living creatures. This means that birds are considered to be ancestors, and butterflies and birds are both common motifs in Miao embroidery.

Traditionally, the hundred-bird gown is made up of more than a dozen sections and takes between three and five years to finish. The fabric features patterns made using a variety of colourful silk threads, with each pattern representing the form of a bird. Some patterns are abstract and others geometric, and the style for men and women is different. Each piece of the hundred-bird gown tells an ancestral legend – it is essentially a Miao epic worn on the body. Embellished with feathers and a variety of silver ornaments, including collars and necklaces, the gown is a truly exquisite adornment that may be passed down through many generations before it is finally buried with an elder, to be returned to its creators.

Top right: Elders in deep blue gowns play the *lusheng* – a central feature of major Miao festivals. **Leishan, Guizhou, 2006**

Above: Miao elders wear these magnificent garments to greet their ancestors in death. **Rongjiang County, Guizhou. Photo: Du Dianwen**

Miao people wearing the hundred-bird gown perform a sacrificial dance during the Guzhang Festival, an ancestor-worship ceremony. Rongjiang County, Guizhou. Photo: Du Dianwen

Falling Leaves Return to Their Roots

Since ancient times, people have placed their greatest hopes in the future but consigned their most precious treasures to the dead. Much of our interpretation of and insight into history comes from artefacts found in tombs.

At Hani burials, a ritual involving shells must be observed: the eldest daughter of the deceased brings out the shells that the deceased either inherited or acquired in life, and the eldest son then places them in the grave. As shells are the most common decoration used for Hani traditional clothing, these will help to identify the deceased as a member of the Hani ethnic group in the afterlife.

Shells were also customarily used by many ancient cultures in Yunnan as a form of contract or currency, and archaeologists have discovered a large number of shell containers dating back to the Bronze Age. Although shells no longer function as money in present-day Yunnan, they are still treasured as jewellery in Hani folklore. It could even be said that they still fulfil their contractual role: acting as an intermediary, an agreement between life and death, between the mortal and the spiritual.

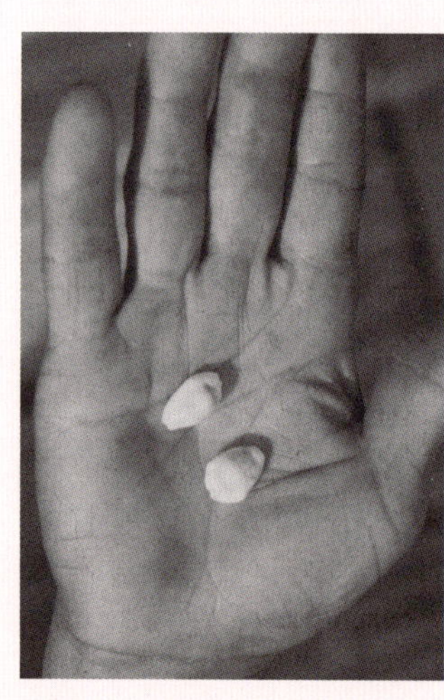

As Hani mourners arrive at the cemetery, the eldest daughter of the deceased hands shells to the eldest son to place in the grave.
Honghe, Yunnan, 1998

Bone Hairpin

In 2001, when I visited a Li village in Hainan, China's southern island province, I learned of a kind of bone hairpin used as a local funeral object. The hairpin is made of animal leg bones or ribs, with black carved lines creating the silhouette of a human with one or two heads, adorned with tall headdresses, headscarves or buns. Other engravings on the hairpin feature animals, plants, waves, swirls and geometric or dot patterns. According to Li folk legend, the human form depicts a Li hero called Gong Ga, a brave and well-respected ancient Li leader who now represents the power of the clan. People wear these hairpins with his image to show respect for the ancestors.

In the past, Li men wore their hair long and secured it with a bone hairpin. Later, as men's hairstyles changed, they no longer used these hairpins themselves, so when a man fell in love with a woman, he would give her a hairpin as a token of his affection. Today, Li women wear clothing and accessories in a mix of ethnic traditions and Western styles. Nevertheless, they will don their traditional Li clothing with a bone hairpin for important occasions such as weddings, funerals and festivals. Every woman has a collection of hairpins, each with its own story to tell. The bone hairpins of the deceased must be broken before they ascend to heaven, lest they be stolen in the afterlife.

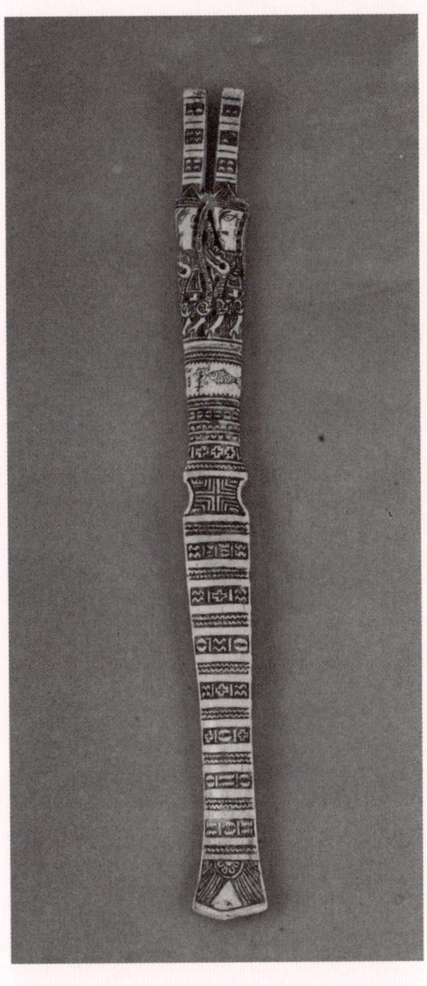
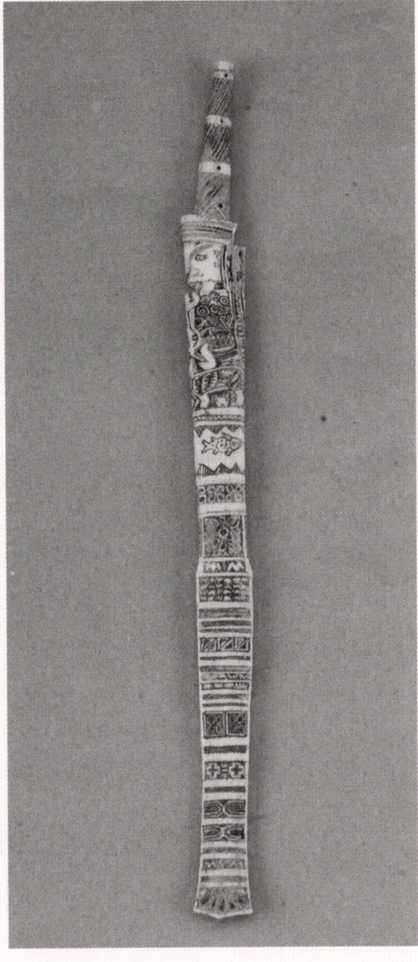
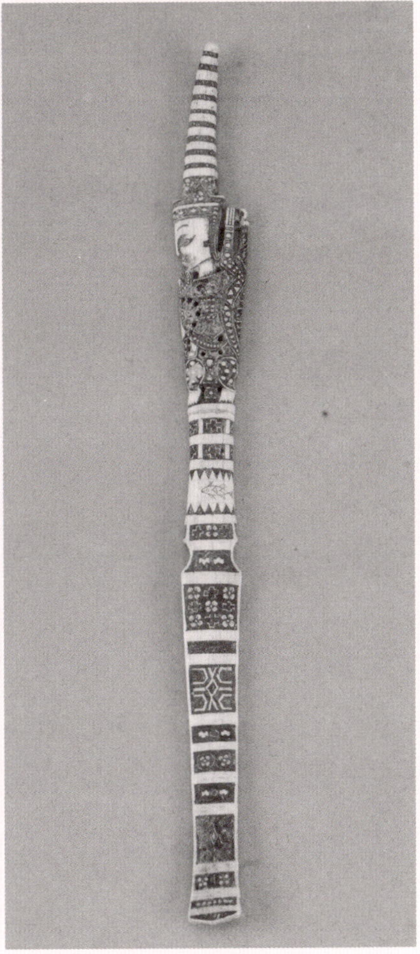

Li bone hairpins. **Guangdong Folk Art Museum, Guangzhou, Guangdong, 1980**

Falling Leaves Return to Their Roots

Flying Bird, Soaring Spirit

Deep in the mountains of Yunnan's Cangyuan Wa Autonomous County, hidden high up on cliffs, are some of the oldest rock paintings in China. Estimated to be more than 3000 years old, the Cangyuan rock paintings were sketched onto the limestone cliffs using a mix of local hematite powder and animal-blood pigments. More than 1000 images have been identified so far, including people, animals, houses, trees and the sun. The scenes mostly depict hunting and gathering, but also dancing and fighting.

When I first saw them with my own eyes, in 1991, the images that puzzled me most were the figures drawn with wings. *Were these gods or holy men, and why did they decorate themselves with feathers and wing-like adornments?* I wondered.

Through extensive research since then, I have found that many ethnic groups maintain a belief that the flying bird is a messenger of the soul. Historical mentions appear in classics like the southern shamanic songs of *Chuci*, attributed to the poet Qu Yuan (c. 340–278 BCE), in which the turtle-dove appears as a messenger between the living and the dead, the mortal and the spirit worlds.

The custom of 'soul-sending' feather adornments is still prevalent today among many ethnic groups in China's south-west, who use 'flying bird' ceremonies and feather accessories to symbolise the transmission of souls to the afterlife. For example, the Pumi and the Naxi wear pheasant tails during funeral processions, Yi priests adorn themselves with eagle talons for burials, and Jingpo shamans wear headdresses decorated with long feathers for funerals and place an engraving of a flying bird into the grave. In Tibetan sky burials, the deceased is placed on a mountaintop, where vultures descend to eat their remains, and the soul rises in flight with the birds.

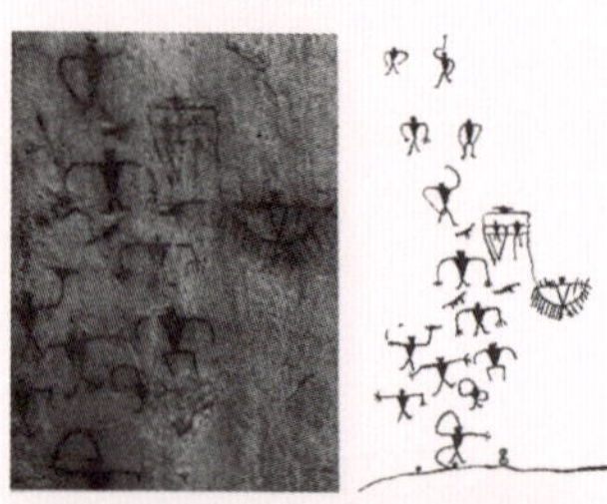

Above: Rock paintings at Cangyuan. **Cangyuan County, 1991**

Top left: A Miao priest in robes and headdress unfolds an ancestral scroll during an ancestor worship ceremony. Xiangxi, Hunan, 2007. Photo: Shi Wei

Top middle and right: Headdress and sceptre of a Naxi *dongba* (priest). Lijiang, Yunnan, 1996

Middle: Crowns and ritual implements of *bimo*, or Yi priests. Chuxiong, Yunnan. Photo: Liu Jianhua

Bottom left and middle: The crown and eagle claws are important for a *bimo* ritual. Dayao County, Yunnan, 1991

Bottom right: Yi elder's clothing and adornments. Shiping County, Yunnan. Photo: Liu Jianhua

The Silver Pheasant

Between 1991 and 1998, I spent time with the Hani people in the Honghe region of Yunnan, researching funeral customs. According to Hani legend, long ago a silver pheasant rescued their dying ancestors and brought them back to life. Therefore, during funeral processions, Hani people perform the silver-pheasant dance to give thanks and to pray for the pheasant to bless the reincarnations of the dead.

Classic texts describe the use of bird imagery in Hani funerals dating back to the Qianlong period (1735–1796). At the modern-day Hani funerals I attended, participants beat bamboo tubes while humming ancient spiritual songs. Several dancers wearing masks performed the lion dance to expel evil spirits, before one of them, dressed as a silver pheasant, started using his mouth to remove the belongings of the deceased, picking them up one by one and placing them in front of the coffin.

During the procession, the coffin – painted with birds and trees – passed through every crossroads in the village, where people stopped to bang on drums and watch as two dancers, with fans as wings, imitated the flight of the silver pheasant. After arriving at the cemetery, they placed a wooden flying bird statue in front of the tomb to complete the funeral rites, sending the deceased's soul to the spiritual realm.

Masked lion dances are performed to exorcise evil spirits at Hani funerals. Honghe, Yunnan, 1991

Top to bottom: After Hani people are buried in a coffin, a bamboo pole with wooden carvings of birds is placed at the grave. **Honghe, Yunnan, 1998;** At every fork in the road, Hani mourners stop and perform a palm-fan dance, imitating the flight of birds to send off the spirit of the deceased. **Honghe, Yunnan, 1998;** A silver pheasant painted on a Hani coffin. **Honghe, Yunnan, 1991**

Falling Leaves Return to Their Roots

Above: Zhuang Daoist leader at a funeral.
Longlin County, Guangxi. Photo: Liang Hanchang

Left and below: Black–Clothes Zhuang funeral.
Napo County, Guangxi, 2008. Photo: Liang Hanchang

Below, top and bottom: Tunpu funeral. **Tunpu, Guizhou, 2006. Photo: Xiong Xun**

Above, top and middle: Baiku Yao funeral. **Nandan, Guangxi, 2009. Photo: Liang Hanchang**

Above, bottom: Because the deceased had a good life, the funeral was a happy occasion. **Nandan, Guangxi, 2009. Photo: Xu Liyu**

Top and middle rows: At the Munao Festival, wearing long gowns and feathered headdresses, local *dongsa* (priests) lead their fellow Jingpo people in a dance symbolising a return to ancestral lands. **Dehong, Yunnan, 1993**

Bottom: Bronze drums at a Yi funeral. The pattern on the drums is similar to that used on batik clothing. **Wenshan, Yunnan, 1988**

Funeral Drums

The bronze drum is essential to the funerals of the Yi, Miao and Bouyei ethnic groups, metaphorically ferrying the souls of the newly deceased and guiding their way to the underworld. In Guangxi and Yunnan, among other regions, bronze drums and copper vessels excavated by archaeologists depict feathered people on boats.

In the past, these images have been interpreted as dragon boats (long wooden rowing boats, often used in races) but, upon closer inspection, the bow and stern of the boats more closely resemble a bird's beak and tail. Flying-bird designs abound on mast and hull. On these mysterious boats, people and objects are drawn in an exaggerated and mutated fashion, with decorations that can include a mast of bird feathers or a perch for a spirit bird. The people have huge feathers on their bodies and heads; some appear to row, some play the *lusheng* (a traditional reed instrument) and others dance. These bird-shaped craft appear to be the boats that transport the deceased's souls to the next world.

Top and left: A bronze drum from the Western Han Dynasty (206 BCE–25 CE) decorated with feathered people on a flying-bird boat. **Guangxi Zhuang Autonomous Region Museum, Nanning, Guangxi, 2014**

Bottom: Baiku Yao mourners beat drums at a funeral. **Nandan, Guangxi, 2008. Photo: Liang Hanchang**

Falling Leaves Return to Their Roots

Previous and above: A Hani Aini woman in Mangjia Village, Xishuangbanna Dai Autonomous Prefecture, Yunnan. Her hands are stained from dying hemp with indigo.

The Fabric of Life and Death

By Suvi Rautio

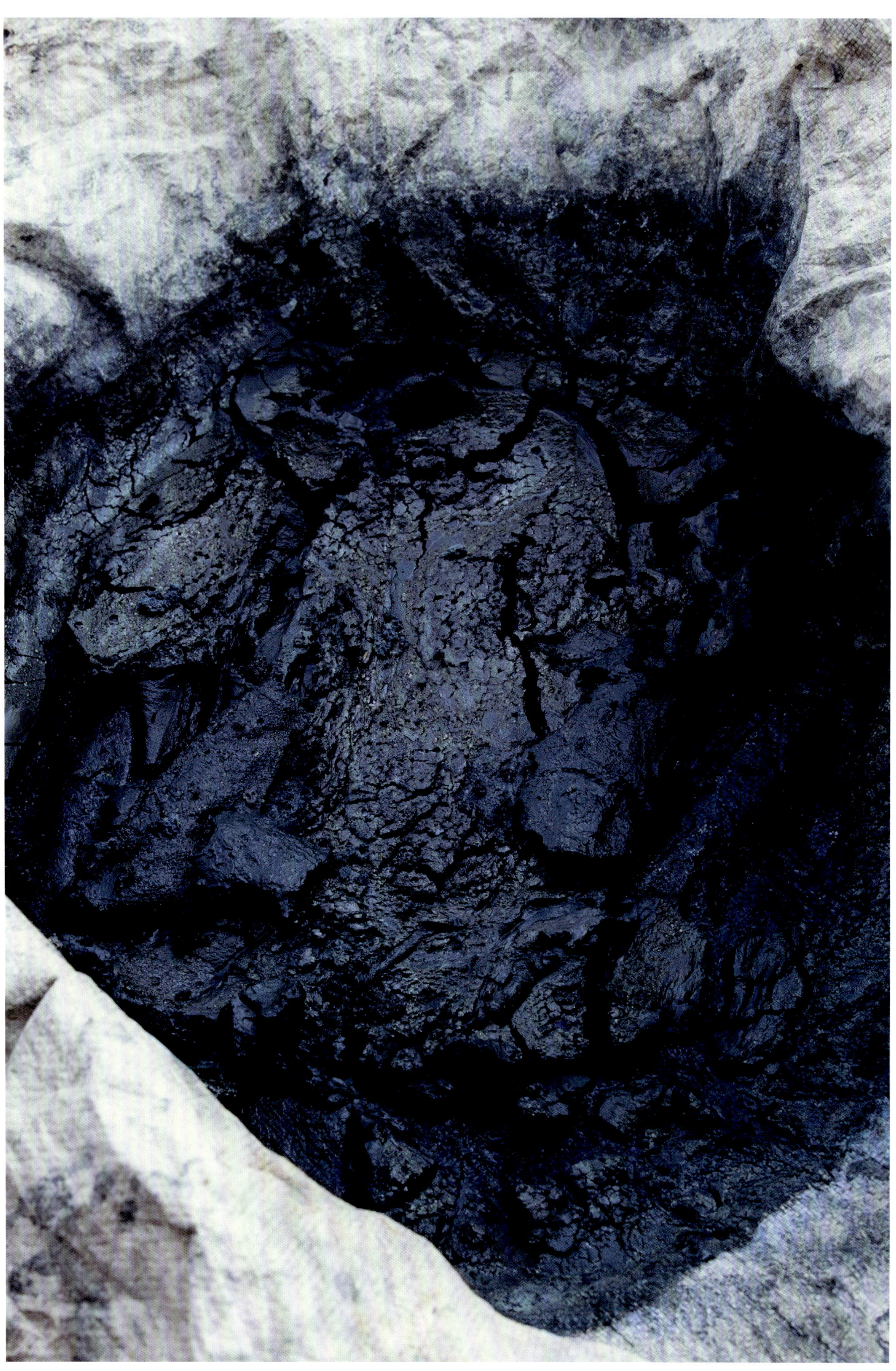

Auntie Yang prepares her indigo-dye bath in the eighth month of the Chinese lunar calendar, when the leaves and stalks of her farmed indigo plants are fermented in alkaline solution. Then, alcohol is added, but only sparingly; otherwise, Auntie Yang jokes, it will exhaust the dye bath, and, just like a human, it will feel sluggish and hungover the following day. The indigo bath is then aerated and activated by pouring and mixing the water until a blue foam starts to bubble up to the surface, and it eventually becomes a paste. Auntie Yang is careful not to use too much strength to stir: excessive force will deplete the dye's energy source and produce inconsistent shades of blue. Once the mixture has been left to settle, the cloth is plunged and soaked in the dye bath, and then hung outside to drip-dry and soak in the soft rays of the morning sun. This is repeated daily until the indigo dye has penetrated the fabric to transform it from an initial shade of green into the favoured dark navy blue.

Situated in a deep valley that carves through the mountainous terrain of south-eastern Guizhou Province, Auntie Yang's village boasts cool weather conditions that are ideal for making high-quality indigo dye, a tradition passed down through generations of Dong women. Indigo is unique in the way it sits and breathes on the outside of each thread. Dyers such as Auntie Yang work with the fluid energy of the pigment, in a way that has an inexplicable element of wonder and magic. At each stage of preparing and handling the contents of the indigo bath, this energy seems to align with the dyer's body to establish a connection between person and fabric. The energy of the dye bath is seen as analagous to the womb, drawing on magical qualities of the female body to produce the required colour of divine blue. If the womb is carrying a foetus, the energy of the dye bath will be ruined, which is why pregnant women are restricted from coming close to the bath.

Once the fabric turns a consistent shade of blue, it is tailored into everyday wear. In the village, middle-aged and older women in particular still wear indigo blouses, designed with a long, loose cut, outlined by clasped knot buttons from the collar down the side of the body, and decorated with colourful stitching at the wrists. Although Dong clothing is less elaborate than the more ornamental attire of other ethnic minorities in the region, the simplicity of the minimal design offers elegance and functionality.

To produce fabric worthy of ceremonial wear to mark life milestones, such as marriage and death, the cloth enters a second phase of dyeing with cowhide extract. Once the cloth has been repeatedly soaked in the extract and hung out to dry, a consistent shine is induced by calendering the fabric with a heavy wooden mallet on a flat stone. With each deliberate pound, a brighter glossy sheen is produced and the material stiffens. The outcome is a captivating cloth, in a dark hue with a glimmering purple-red effect; when worn, the cloth stands away from the body.

In the Dong cultural framework, being able to produce dazzling fabric that warrants display is a measure of value and reputation for both wearers and their families. For example, if a man has Dong attire with a remarkably beautiful glossy sheen, it conveys to others that he is married to a competent wife. Insider knowledge informs the value of the sheen and the competency of the dyer's handiwork, which can easily go unnoticed to the untrained eye.

So valued are textiles that they serve as currency at the gates of the underworld to pay back one's life debts – a vital act to ensure a smoother journey from the world of the living. In Auntie Yang's village, only handmade textiles prepared by female kin are worthy of clothing the dead. The role taken on by daughters or – in the absence of daughters – sisters in weaving and dyeing the finest-quality fabric for a person's final change of dress is an expression of love and care that binds the giver and the receiver. First, bundles of handmade textiles are prepared, woven with cotton thread on narrow looms. This white cotton is then dyed with natural indigo, creating a bond between the maker – specifically her life-giving womb, symbolised by the dye bath – and the dead.

Only time will tell how long Dong people will continue dressing the dead in traditional handmade garments, but, for now, women such as Auntie Yang spend mornings nourishing their indigo dye with the utmost precision and care, as if bathing a breathing body. Although textiles remain an integral part of life for the Dong people, the practice of passing down textile traditions – such as weaving, indigo dyeing and embroidery – is becoming increasingly rare. This decline can be attributed to broader social changes since the 1980s, when China started to experience one of the largest migrations in human history. The pull of migrant labour from the countryside to coastal urban centres is felt strongly in the more economically disadvantaged regions of China's south-western periphery, such as Guizhou.

Given the decline in the number of year-round residents in Auntie Yang's village, few villagers now have the interest or the time to commit to labour-intensive textile traditions. It is not just anyone who can learn these arts; they are traditionally passed down exclusively within the Dong community through oral instruction.

As well as watching Auntie Yang dye her textiles, I observed many other women in the village partake in other textile traditions, including warp-faced weaving and embroidery. They made narrow belts and apron bands, and crafted braided trims to be hand sewn onto the hems of shirts. I particularly admired the elaborate flower and butterfly designs embroidered with colourful threads on carrier slings and hats for babies.

In recent years, tourists and designers travelling through the region have revived interest in local handicrafts. These encounters have amplified the commercial value of Dong textiles and created new markets, nationally and even globally. Designers capitalise on the knowledge of Dong women to add new aesthetic elements to their products.

At the same time, in the village, the accessibility of cheap fabrics has made it less desirable to produce traditional adornments. Rural dwellers across China face pressure to leave home to make money in the cities. Many who opt to stay cater to tourists by selling inexpensive, generic wholesale costumes that feed a certain trope of ethnicity. Only a few surviving local women still know how to work with traditional textiles to produce fabric and adornments for everyday and ceremonial wear. Maintaining textile traditions requires diligence and patience from both the teacher and receiver of knowledge. And for ceremonial textiles, it also requires continuity in Dong beliefs and the rituals that feature these textiles.

I studied indigo dyeing and embroidery over the course of thirteen months between 2015 and 2018, while conducting research on heritage initiatives and rural development in a Dong village in Guizhou.

Previous: Bailuo Yi women in
hand-embroidered traditional
dress at a festival in Chengzhai
Village, Wenshan Zhuang and Miao
Autonomous Prefecture, Yunnan.

Opposite: A Hani Aini cow-bone
ornament from a festival headdress,
Mangjia Village, Yunnan.

Following: Kham Tibetan sisters
spinning prayer wheels during Tibetan
new year celebrations in Dege
County, Garze Tibetan Autonomous
Prefecture, Sichuan.

This spread: A Bailuo Yi man in traditional clothes at a festival in Chengzhai Village, Yunnan.

Following: De'ang women dressed for a festival in Padangba Village, Dehong Dai and Jingpo Autonomous Prefecture, Yunnan.

Opposite: An elderly De'ang woman dressed for a festival in Padangba Village, Yunnan.

Right: A Miao woman at Laomeng market, Honghe Hani and Yi Autonomous Prefecture, Yunnan.

Previous left: A Hani Aini woman
wearing cow-bone ornaments
in her festival headdress in
Mangjia Village, Yunnan.

Previous right: A Dai woman
playing a gong at a festival
in Mandan Village, Dehong
Dai and Jingpo Autonomous
Prefecture, Yunnan.

Opposite: The oldest man
in the Flowery Yi village of
Daping, Wenshan Zhuang
and Miao Autonomous
Prefecture, Yunnan.

Above: An older River Miao man
rows a boat traditionally used
for trade along the Qingshui River,
Shidong Town, Qiandongnan
Miao and Dong Autonomous
Prefecture, Guizhou.

Opposite: Foliage near
Basha Village, Qiandongnan
Miao and Dong Autonomous
Prefecture, Guizhou.

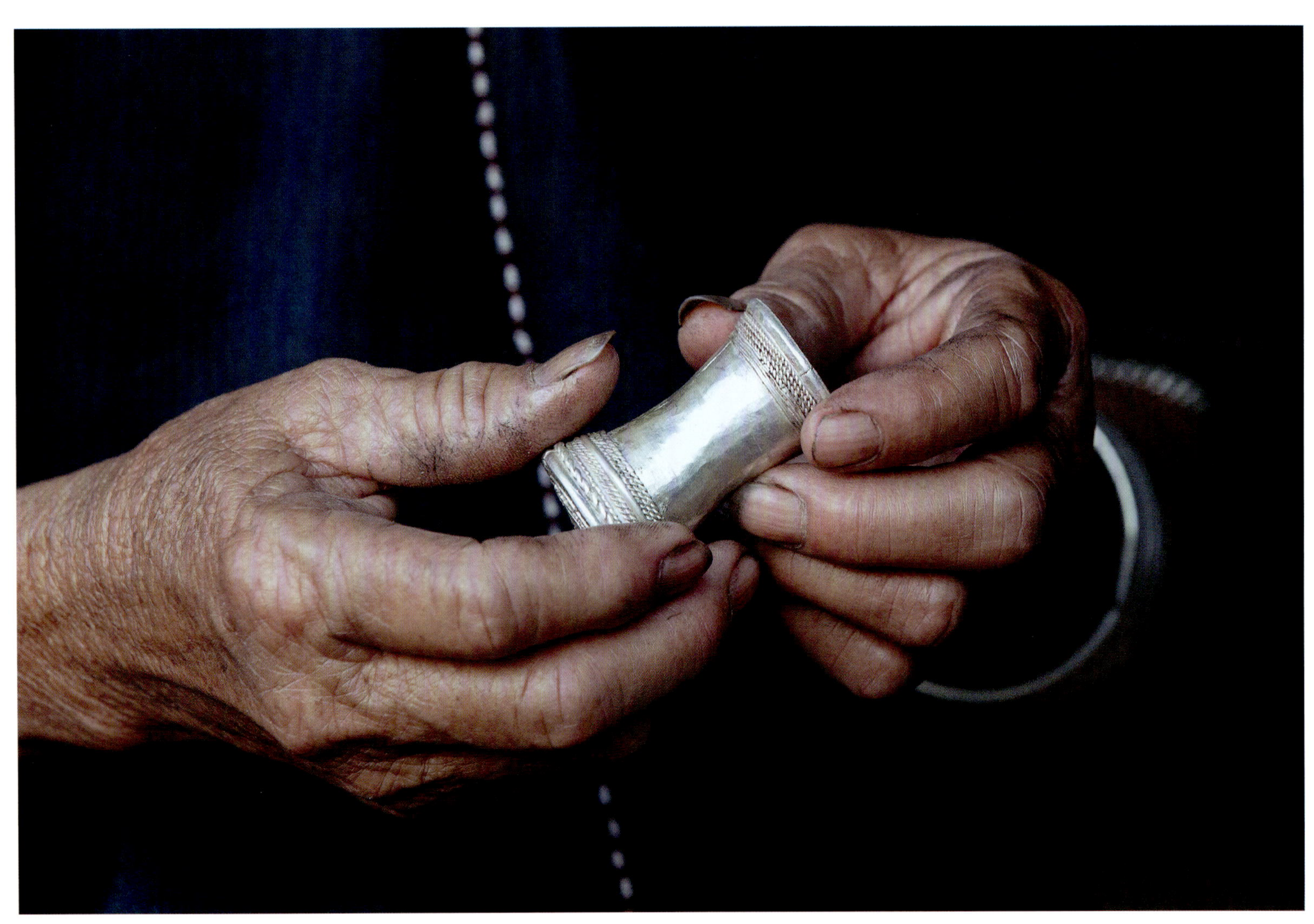

This spread: An older Wa woman with a traditional earpiece, Xishuangbanna Dai Autonomous Prefecture, Yunnan.

Following: A view of the Qingshui River in Shidong Town, Guizhou.

This spread: An elderly Kham Tibetan woman wearing a traditional *chuba*, handmade yak-skin boots and coral and turquoise hair ornaments at Dzongsar Monastery, Dege County, Sichuan.

Previous right: The Duoyishu rice terraces at sunset in Yuanyang County, Honghe Hani and Yi Autonomous Prefecture, Yunnan Province.

Previous left and oposite: An elderly Hani Aini woman with a headdress covered in silverbaubles, showing that she has become a grandmother, in Mangjia Village, Yunnan.

Above: Raw hemp fibre being spun into yarn in Mangjia Village, Yunnan.

Opposite: Hand-spun hemp yarn in the Hani Aini village of Mangjia, in Yunnan. The yarn will be woven on a loom and hand-dyed to make colourful fabric.

Jingpo elderly man, at a
1 year naming ceromony,
Yunnan Province.

Above: Hani men at a festival street banquet in a village near the Duoyishu rice terraces, Yuanyang County, Honghe Hani and Yi Autonomous Prefecture, Yunnan.

Opposite: A Yi funeral procession through Danuohei Village, Shilin Yi Autonomous County, Yunnan.

A Miao woman at Laomeng
market, Yunnan.

An elderly De'ang woman at a festival
in Padangba Village, Yunnan.

Opposite: De'ang people in Padangba Village, Yunnan.

Following: Mountains around Padangba Village, Yunnan.

Miao men once free climbed sheer cliffs over rivers to hang coffins, which can still be seen suspended high above the water in and around Swallow Cave, in Getu River National Park, Ziyun Miao and Buyei Autonomous County, Guizhou. Now, Miao people free climb to collect rare medicinal herbs for asthma and rheumatism that grow high up on the cliff walls.

A Basha Miao elder and young boy
holding rifles – traditionally used to
hunt wild pigs, rabbits and birds –
in Basha Village, Guizhou.

Bailuo Yi woman's festival dress
in Chengzhai Village, Yunnan.

This spread: A grandmother from
a Four-Seal Miao family grazing
her herd of cattle in the mountains,
all the while spinning yarn from
homegrown hemp in Qiaoliang
Village, Liuzhi County, Guizhou
Province. Her skirt is also made from
woven hemp fabric, pleated and
embellished with a batik design.

Opposite: An older Kham Tibetan woman adorned with coral and turquoise at Dzongsar Monastery in Dege County, Sichuan.

Above: Dege Scripture Printing House is at the heart of Tibetan literary heritage, housing over 200,000 printing blocks from classics of Tibetan Buddhism, history, medicine, art and mathematics.

Previous: A Hani Aini grandmother cooking in her home in Mangjia Village, Yunnan. Women cover their legs between the ankle and the knee as protection from snakes.

Opposite: A Hani Aini grandmother working m the field in Mangjia Village, Yunnan.

An elderly Wa Woman
with traditional earpiece,
silver jewellery and pipe,
Xishuangbanna Dai Autonomous
Prefecture, Yunnan Province.

An elderly Hani woman in Yuanyang
County, Yunnan.

Photograph

Appendix

Textiles and embroidery

This spread: Bailuo Yi

357

358

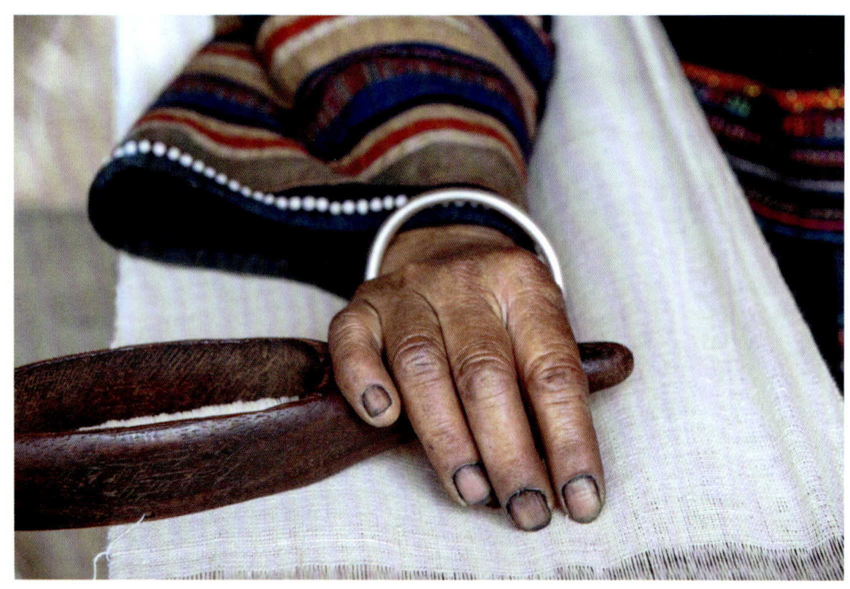

This spread: Hani Aini

Above: River Miao

Opposite page: Four-Seal Miao

This spread: Four-Seal Miao

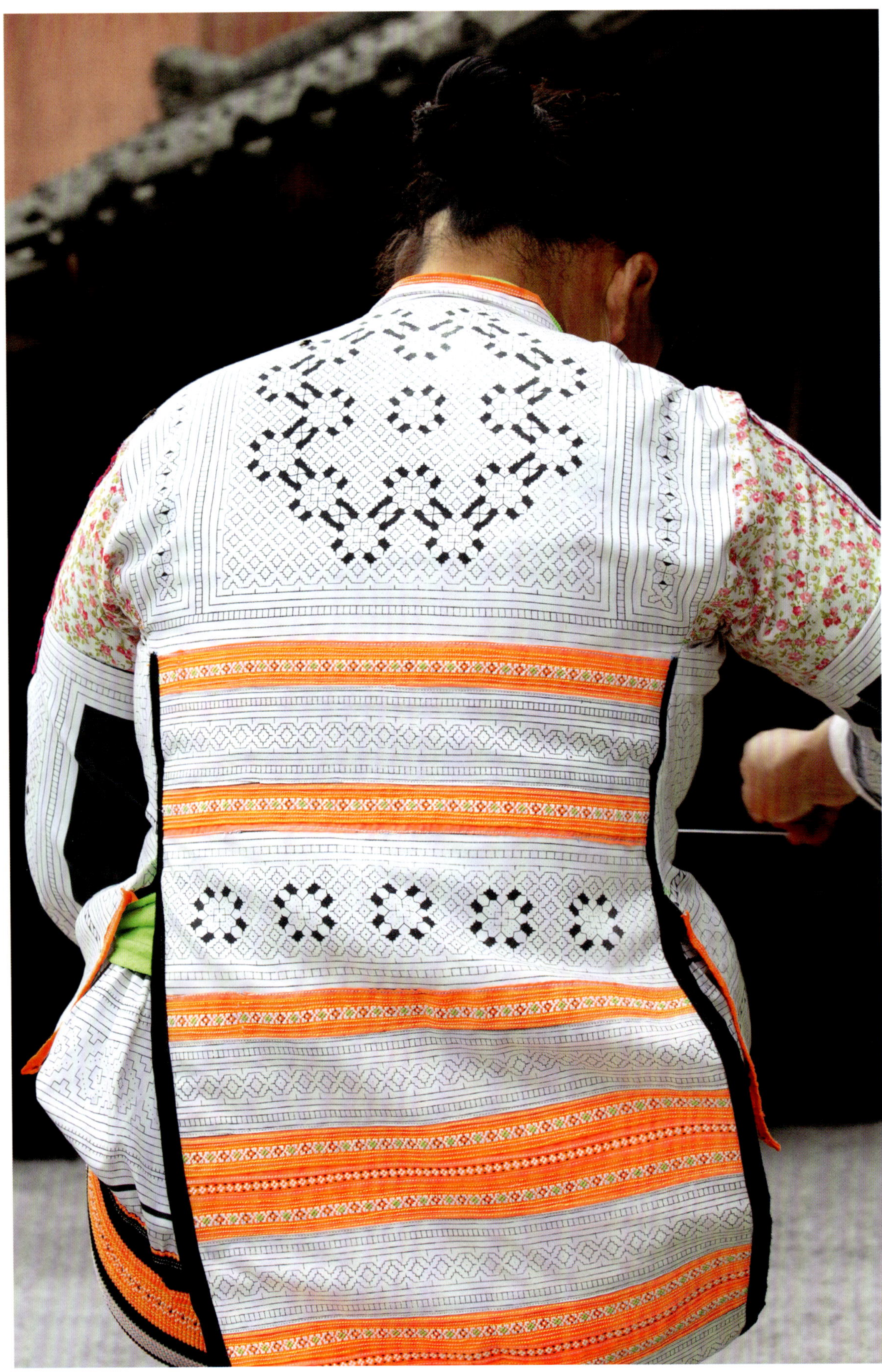

This spread: Longhorn Miao

Basket ware and weaving

This spread: Hani Aini

Basha Miao

Hani Aini

Opposite, top and bottom left:
Longhorn Miao

Opposite, bottom right:
Four-Seal Maio

Above: Longhorn Miao

Kham Tibetan

Longhorn Miao

Dwellings and temples

This spread:
Tibetan temple

This page: Bai

This page: Kham Tibetan

This page: Jiabang Miao

Right: Wudong Village

Below: Dai

Opposite: River Miao

Left column, top to bottom: Basha Miao; Baibei Miao; Dai

Right column, top to bottom: Basha Miao; Baibei Miao; Bailuo Yi

Opposite page: River Miao

This page: Yiche

389

This spread: Getu River –
High Mountain Miao

390

End

Afterword

By Xue Xinran

My husband, Toby Eady, and I watched the Beijing 2008 Summer Olympics opening ceremony at our London flat. When the colourful traditional costumes of China's fifty-six ethnic groups filled the stadium stage, Toby made an observation: the world's understanding of Chinese ethnic minority culture was almost blank. He was awed by the obviously rich traditions that informed the adornments. It would be terrible, he said to me, if rapid modernisation were to destroy these brilliant, ancient cultural legacies.

The next morning, over our daily green tea, we continued the conversation: what a pity that the folklore and tradition of so many communities around the world lives on in daily ritual practices – yet this knowledge remains obscured by ignorance and language barriers, and goes unrecognised in the writing of world history. By the time we started on breakfast – our table laden with Russian bread and French jam, Greek yoghurt with Spanish fruit, Italian coffee with local British milk – we had decided to produce a book by a Chinese author to introduce China's diverse ethnic dress and adornment to the world.

Toby had championed a similar book in the 1980s titled *Africa Adorned*, when he was agent for renowned photographers Angela Fisher and Carol Beckwith. It took us more than six years to find the perfect author for the new project. In that time, we travelled to China more than twice each year to meet candidates and hear their visions for the book. We sifted through thousands upon thousands of photographs. Yet Toby instinctively knew that no one was a perfect match – until we met Professor Deng Qiyao in Guangzhou in 2014. The professor had devoted thirty years to finding and recording ancient folklore, traditional adornments and family histories from China's ethnic groups. When we spoke at his office in the Department of Anthropology at Sun Yat-sen University, the passion he had cultivated since his twenties shone through.

The next three years were spent laying the foundations for *China Adorned*. When Toby passed away on 24 December 2017, he and Professor Deng had already created a bright future for this remarkable book, fuelled by their shared passion, nonstop conversation and devotion to preserving the world's cultures.

My darling Toby, we are now able to share your beloved *China Adorned* with the world, as you wished. Thank you for giving the book your hope and your heart.

394

Bibliography

All citations refer to Chinese-language texts unless otherwise noted. Original publication dates are noted where relevant. Author surnames appear in all capitals.

CAO Xueqin and GAO E, *Hónglóu mèng* (Dream of the Red Chamber), People's Literature Publishing House, Beijing, 1982 (Qing Dynasty, 1636–1912).

CHEN Shou, 'Wèi zhì dōng yí zhuàn' (The Eastern Barbarians, Records of the Wei), *Sānguó zhì* (Records of Three Kingdoms), Shanghai Ancient Books Publishing House, Shanghai, 1986 (Western Jin Dynasty, 266–316).

DENG Qiyao and ZHANG Liu (eds), *Mìjìng jié jì* (Festivals in the Mysterious Land of Yunnan), Yunnan People's Publishing House, Kunming, 1991.

DENG Qiyao and DU Xinyan (eds), *Zhōngguó xībù mínzú jié rìzhì* (The Festivals of Western China), Yunnan University Press, Kunming, 2019.

FANG Guoyu (ed.), *Yúnnán shǐliào cóngkān* (Yunnan Historical Series), Yunnan University Press, Kunming, 1998, vol. 13.

LIU Xiaobing, 'Hún zhōu, chuán guān yǔ chén mù shénhuà' (The Myth of the Soul Boat, Boat Coffin and Driftwood), thesis published for the fourth International Thai Society Study, Kunming, 1990.

MEAD Margaret, *Sàmóyǎ rén de chéngnián* (Coming of Age in Samoa), trans. ZHOU Xiaohong, LI Yaojun and LIU Jing, The Commercial Press, Beijing, 2008.

National Bureau of Statistics of China, 'Tabulation on the 2010 Population Census of the People's Republic of China', China Statistical Press, Beijing, 2012, <www.stats.gov.cn/english/Statisticaldata/CensusData/rkpc2010/indexch.htm> (in English).

QU Dajun, *Guǎngdōng xīn yǔ* (Historical Notes on Guangdong), Zhonghua Book Company, Beijing, 1997 (Qing Dynasty, 1636–1912).

YAN Ruxian and SONG Zhaolin, *Yǒngníng Nàxī zú de mǔxì zhì* (The Matrilineal System of the Yongning Naxi), Yunnan People's Publishing House, Kunming, 1983.

ZHAN Chengxu, WANG Chengquan, LI Jinchun and LIU Longchu, *Yǒngníng Nàxī zú de ā zhù hūnyīn hé mǔxì jiātíng* (The Azhu Marriage and Matrilineal Family of the Yongning Naxi), Shanghai People's Publishing House, Shanghai, 1980.

Zhōngguó gè mínzú zōngjiào yǔ shénhuà dà cídiǎn (Encyclopaedia of the Religions and Myths of Chinese Ethnic Groups), Xueyuan Publishing House, Beijing, 1990.

ZHOU Mingqi and LI Renfan (eds), *Zhōngguó gè mínzú nián jié jì huì dàshì diǎn* (Encyclopaedia of the Festivals of Chinese Ethnic Groups), Shaanxi People's Education Press, Xi'an, 1995.

Contributors

Professor Deng Qiyao is the Director and Guest Professor of the Visual Culture Research Center of the Guangzhou Academy of Fine Arts and the honorary Vice Chairman of the China Adventure Association. His previous positions include Director of, and active researcher at, the Institute of Ethnic Literature of the Yunnan Academy of Social Sciences and Professor at the School of Sociology and Anthropology of Sun Yat-Sen University.

Cat Vinton is an adventure and ethnographic photographer documenting ways of life – unobtrusively photographing the nomadic and Indigenous peoples of the world. She has been published in *National Geographic* online, the *Guardian*, Survival International, *Oceanographic Magazine*, *Sirene Journal* and *Sidetracked Magazine*. Photography is Cat's part in the storytelling of life, encouraging people to reconnect to the land and community, and to be a part of protecting our natural world and all the ways of life that coexist.

Xue Xinran is a British-Chinese journalist, author and speaker, with a particular focus on women's issues. She is a regular contributor to the *Guardian*, the BBC and CNN, and has published eight books internationally, including *The Good Women of China*, *Sky Burial* and *The Promise: Love and Loss in Modern China*.

Wu Fan is the author of two novels, *February Flowers* and *Beautiful as Yesterday*. Currently living in the United States, Wu writes in both English and Chinese and has had short stories published in *Granta* and *Ploughshares*, among other publications.

Will Spence is a professional translator with a range of China-focused experience, from consulting for British and Chinese businesses to news and literary translation.

Acknowledgements

This book is dedicated to Toby Eady, whose research beginning in 2008 laid the foundations for this project.

The publisher would like to thank everyone who made *China Adorned* possible, including:

Xie Shanqing, Wang Yuqiang
    and the Yilin Press team
Liu Haochong (Leo) and Wang Ruiling (Linda)
The Mothers' Bridge of Love team
The Sino-UK Culture Bridge team

Index

Opposite: An ethnic Tibetan family on their way to the temple in Hongkor, Bayan Har Mountains, Qinghai. The family are Kham Tibetans – or Khampa, meaning nomads from the Kham region – and live along the Qinghai–Sichuan border. Khampa women often wear jewellery made from turquoise and coral, while Khampa men wear their hair long, with a red or black tassel woven in, and often earrings.

First published in Australia in 2022
by Thames & Hudson Australia Pty Ltd
11 Central Boulevard, Portside Business Park
Port Melbourne, Victoria 3207
ABN: 72 004 751 964

First published in the United Kingdom in 2022
By Thames & Hudson Ltd
181a High Holborn
London WC1V 7QX

First published in the United States of America in 2023
By Thames & Hudson Inc.
500 Fifth Avenue
New York, New York 10110

China Adorned © Thames & Hudson Australia 2022

Text © Deng Qiyao
Images © remains with the individual copyright holders

25 24 23 22   5 4 3 2 1

Thames & Hudson Australia wishes to acknowledge that
Aboriginal and Torres Strait Islander people are the first
storytellers of this nation and the traditional custodians of
the land on which we live and work. We acknowledge their
continuing culture and pay respect to Elders past, present
and future.

ISBN 978-1-760-76058-8 (hardback)
ISBN 978-1-760-76301-5 (U.S. edition)

A catalogue record for this
book is available from the
National Library of Australia

British Library Cataloguing-in-Publication Data
A catalogue record for this book is available from the
British Library

Library of Congress Control Number 2022932725

Every effort has been made to trace accurate ownership
of copyrighted text and visual materials used in this book.
Errors or omissions will be corrected in subsequent editions,
provided notification is sent to the publisher.

Front cover:
Photo by Cat Vinton

Design: Ashlea O'Neill, Salt Camp Studio
Editing: Xue Xinran and Alison Cowan
Printed and bound in China by C&C Offset Printing Co., Ltd

FSC® is dedicated to the promotion of responsible forest
management worldwide. This book is made of material from
FSC®-certified forests and other controlled sources.

Be the first to know about our new releases,
exclusive content and author events by visiting
thamesandhudson.com.au
thamesandhudson.com
thamesandhudsonusa.com